T0268215

Habibti Driver

By Shamia Chalabi & Sarah Henley

Habibti Driver was first produced by Tara Finney Productions in an
earlier version – *Burkas and Bacon Butties* – at VAULT Festival, London,
in 2018. This revised, full-length version premiered at the
Octagon Theatre Bolton in April 2022, co-produced with
Tara Finney Productions.

Habibti Driver

By Shamia Chalabi & Sarah Henley

CAST

Shazia	Shamia Chalabi
Yasmin	Houda Echouafni
Ashraf	Dana Haqjoo
Chris	Timothy O'Hara
Jean	Helen Sheals
Yusuf	Hemi Yeroham

CREATIVE TEAM

Director	Sepy Baghaei
Designer	Helen Coyston
Lighting Designer	Pablo Fernandez Baz
Sound Designer	Dinah Mullen
Movement Director	Jennifer Jackson
Fight Director	Kaitlin Howard
Assistant Director	Sarah Jane Schostack

PRODUCTION TEAM

Producers	Catt Belcher for Octagon Theatre & Tara Finney for Tara Finney Productions
Production Manager	Jack Boissieux
Assistant Producer	Olivia Barr
Company Stage Manager	Lisa Cochrane
Assistant Stage Manager	Caitlin Chatfield
Technical Manager	Kay Buckley
Senior Sound Technician	Matt Masson
Lighting Technician	Kevin Williams
Senior Stage Technician	Philip Thackray
Costume Supervisor	Sarah White
Wardrobe Assistant	Jess Wild
Henna Artist	Nilufar Patel
Set Builders	Footprint Scenery
Additional Carpentry	Ben Cook & Andrew Bubble
Production Technician	Harry Hearne
Community Engagement Officer	Niparun Nessa
Graphic Designer	Steph Pyne
Photography	The Other Richard (Publicity) Colin J Smith (Rehearsal) Pamela Raith (Production)

Supporters

This production would not have been possible without the generous support of Arts Council England.

ARTS COUNCIL
ENGLAND

Thanks

We would also like to thank:

Jerwood Space | Royal Shakespeare Company | Park Theatre | Peggy Ramsay Foundation | Shoreditch Town Hall | Arcola Theatre | Arts Ed | Prime Theatre

The Cast & Crew of *Burkas and Bacon Butties* at VAULT Festival: Sarah Butcher | Jon Everett | Alex Lewer | Tom Rogers | Tiran Aakel | Holly Joyce | Luke Murphy | Lisa Zahra | Tina Dezart | Liam McLaughlin

All our R&D Casts & Crews: Salman Ahktar | Laila Alj | Raj Bajaj | Debra Baker | Sarah Belcher | Michelle Bonnard | Matt Dan | Emilio Doorgasing | Christian Edwards | Waleed Elgadi | Nadi Kemp-Sayfi | Naveed Khan | Ingrid Mackinnon | Yasmin Taheri

CAST

SHAMIA CHALABI – SHAZIA

Theatre credits: *Force Majeure* (Donmar Warehouse); *Tartuffe, Tamburlaine* (Royal Shakespeare Company); *Burkas and Bacon Butties* (Tara Finney Productions/VAULT Festival); *Last Thursday – The Verbatim Project* (The Wyvern Theatre); *Broadcasting Bites* (Leicester Square Theatre); *Alcohol City Lights and Slow Songs* (The Bush Bazaar); *From Where I'm Standing* (DELIRIUM/Edinburgh Underbelly/Pegasus Theatre); *Little Red Riding Headscarf* (Equal Writes/Tristan Bates Theatre).

Television credits: *Coronation Street, Doctors, EastEnders, Law and Order UK, Anti-Social Network.*

HOUDA ECHOUAFNI – YASMIN

Trained: The London Centre of Theatre Studies.

Theatre credits: *A Museum in Bhagdad, King John* (Royal Shakespeare Company); *One Thousand and One Nights* (The Royal Lyceum Theatre); *Dialogues from Babel, The Things I Would Tell You* (Traverse Theatre); *Blackout* (Summerhall); *A Midsummer Night's Dream, The Duchess of Malfi, Three Sisters* (The Actor's Company); *Hassan Lklishe* (Royal Court Theatre); *Return* (Soho Theatre).

Television credits: *Jesus: His life* (History Channel); *Doctors, Sea of Souls, Waking the Dead* (BBC); *Green Wing* (Channel 4); *Hotel Babylon* (ITV): *The Grid* (Fox Network).

Film credits: *I Saved My Bellydancer, Dirty War, Piercing Brightness, Leviathan.*

DANA HAQJOO – ASHRAF

Theatre credits: *The Boy With Two Hearts* (Wales Millennium Centre); *Notmoses* (Arts Centre).

Television credits: *The Ipcress File, Hapless, Tin Star 3, Coronation Street, Deep Water, Deep State, The City and the City, Emmerdale, Tyrant, Citizen Khan, The Bill, The Omid Djalili Show.*

Film credits: *United We Fall, Two For Joy, In Another Life, Amaurosis, Desert Dancer.*

Radio credits: *Welcome to Iran, Miriam and Youssef, Fall of the Shah.*

TIMOTHY O'HARA – CHRIS

Trained: Webber Douglas Academy of Dramatic Art, Central School of Speech and Drama, Moscow Art Theatre School.

Theatre credits: *The Shark Is Broken* (SFP/The Ambassadors Theatre); *The Hardest One* (Bon & Co/The Other Palace); *Little Mermaid* (Pins and Needles/The Egg Bath); *Burkas and Bacon Butties* (Tara Finney Productions/VAULT Festival); *Wretch* (VAULT Festival); *The Mousetrap* (Mousetrap Productions); *The Night Before Christmas* (Different Breed); *None So Blind* (Attic Theatre/Playfest 2015); *Positive Suit* (Theatre503); *Shakespeare in Love* (Noël Coward Theatre); *Scoop* (Pins and Needles/Lyric Hammersmith); *London Wall* (St James Theatre/Finborough Theatre); *Chaire, Have I Non* (Lyric Hammersmith); *Coffin* (King's Head Theatre); *There Will Be More, The Pope's Wedding* (The Cock Tavern); *Getting Away, Getting Out* (Giant Olive).

Television credits: *Casualty.*

Film credits: *Sherlock Holmes* (Guy Richie).

HELEN SHEALS – JEAN

Theatre credits: *Shirley Valentine* (Hamburg); *Brassed Off* (New Vic Theatre); *The Wonderful Wizard of Oz* (Octagon Theatre, Bolton); *Judy and Liza* (Liverpool Royal Court/UK tour); *Judy!* (The Arts Theatre); *The Merry Wives* (Northern Broadsides/ New Vic Theatre); *The Wars of the Roses* (Northern Broadsides/Leeds Playhouse); *Macbeth, Twelfth Night, King Lear, A Midsummer Night's Dream* (Northern Broadsides); *Quasimodo* (King's Head Theatre); *Vieux Carrie* (Charing Cross Theatre); *The Rise and Fall of Little Voice* (Hull Truck Theatre Company); *One Night in November* (Belgrade Theatre); *A Taste of Honey* (Salisbury Playhouse); *Flare Path, Marat/Sade, A Taste of Honey, The Rise and Fall of Little Voice* (Bristol Old Vic); *Cabaret* (Live Theatre) and seasons at the RSC.

Television credits: *Coronation Street, Doctors, Brookside, The Hello Girl, Family Affairs, Dalziel and Pascoe, Metrosexuality, Holby City, Courtroom, The Bill, Silent Witness, Last Tango in Halifax, Casualty, Downtown Abbey.*

HEMI YEROHAM – YUSUF

Trained: Guildford School of Acting.

Theatre credits: *Berberian Sound Studio* (Donmar Warehouse); *Arabian Nights* (Hoxton Hall); *Alice's Adventures Underground* (Les Enfants Terribles); *Romeo and Juliet, The Adventures of Sherlock Holmes* (US tour & Off-Broadway); *Operation Magic Carpet* (Polka Theatre); *Once Upon a Time* (UK tour); *66 Minutes in Damascus* (LIFT & Theatre of Sao Paulo Biennal); *The Arabian Nights* (Tricycle Theatre); *The Tempest* (Cambridge Shakespeare Festival); *Hate* (Holland tour); *The Cradle Will Rock* (Arcola Theatre); *Shadow Language* (Theatre503); *The Container* (UK tour).

Radio credits: *The Amelia Project, The Long View, Ambridge Extra, Turnpike Lane, Forgiving, The Cool Bag Baby, Poppyseeds.*

Television credits: *The Cockfields, Benidorm, Tyrant, You've Been Served, Sunshine Simon, Bad Grandad, EastEnders E20.*

Film credits: *Closed, Mamma Mia.*

Creative & Production Team

SHAMIA CHALABI – WRITER

Shamia is a London-based actor and writer who trained at Arts Educational School London. She was recently commissioned to write and perform a monologue for Octagon's collaboration with MACFest and hosted a 'Writing Your Life' workshop. *Habibti Driver* is Shamia's first full-length play.

SARAH HENLEY – WRITER

Sarah is a London-based writer, who was listed on the BBC New Talent Hotlist in 2017. She co-founded Burn Bright with Tori Allen-Martin – an organisation that aims to level the playing field for women and women writers. She's also co-founder and Co-CEO of NextUp – a subscription video platform for live comedy.

Sarah was commissioned with Tori Allen-Martin to turn Idris Elba's *mi Mandela* album into a musical, *Tree*, and worked on this extensively for four years, leading it to a workshop at The Dominion Theatre. She was also Writer's Assistant to Jeffrey Lane (Tony Award winner) on the West End production of *Women on the Verge of a Nervous Breakdown*.

She most recently enjoyed the opportunity to write the Christmas show for the Tobacco Factory in Bristol, an adaptation of *The Wizard of Oz*. Her play for Delirium Theatre, *From Where I'm Standing* received five-star reviews and The Stage's 'Must See' badge in Edinburgh. Writing credits include: *Oz, Burkas and Bacon Butties, Getting Out, Getting Away, After the Turn, Cinderella, From Where I'm Standing, Streets* (Offie nomination for Best New Musical and Most Promising Playwright), *Another Way* (Offie nomination for Best New Musical), *Muted* (Offie nomination for Best New Musical), *The Unblinding, Muted* (Offie nominated Best New Musical), *Essence*.

SEPY BAGHAEI – DIRECTOR

Trained: Royal Central School of Speech and Drama; Australian Academy of Dramatic Art.

Directing credits: *Little Women, CITIZEN, Wilde Tales, Mycorrhiza* (The Space); *The Wolf Inside Me* (Blue Elephant Theatre); *Re: Memory* (Suitcase Civilians/UK & Australia tour); *Body Language* (Brave New Word); *Grimm Tales* (City of Sydney/ Sydney Fringe); *Something to Be Done* (Short+Sweet Sydney).

As Staff/Assistant Director: *Manor* (National Theatre); *Once Upon a Time in Nazi Occupied Tunisia* (Almeida); *Welcome to Iran* (Stratford East/National Theatre); *Reasons To Stay Alive* (Sheffield Theatres/English Touring Theatre); *Othello* (English Touring Theatre); *As You Like It* (Regent's Park Open Air Theatre).

Sepy is Co-Vice Chair of MENA Arts UK, Associate Director at The Space, and a board member of Stage Directors UK.

Awards include: Ian Potter Cultural Trust Award; Guildford Academic Associates Scholarship; Best Production (Winner) and Best New Talent (Nominee) for *Something To Be Done* at Short+Sweet Sydney.

HELEN COYSTON – DESIGNER

Trained: Royal Central School of Speech and Drama.

Recent Design credits: *Operation Mincemeat* (New Diorama/Southwark Playhouse); *Home, I'm Darling* (Theatre by the Lake/SJT/Octagon); *Rapunzel, Puss in Boots* (The Theatre Chipping Norton); *Two, Our Mutual Friend* (Hull Truck); *Seeds* (Leeds Playhouse/UK tour); *The Snow Queen, Treasure Island, Stepping Out, Alice in Wonderland* (Scarborough); *A Christmas Carol, The 39 Steps, Build a Rocket* (Stephen Joseph Theatre); *Goth Weekend* (Stephen Joseph Theatre/Live Theatre, Newcastle); *Homing Birds* (Kali Theatre); *Sex with Robots and Other Devices* (King's Head Theatre); *Antigone* (UK tour); *The Acedian Pirates* (Theatre503); *Short Changed* (Theatre Royal Plymouth); *My Mother Said I Never Should* (St James Theatre); *The Musicians* (Royal & Derngate); *Peter Pan, Watership Down, There is a War* (Watford Palace Theatre); *Bluebird* (Edinburgh Fringe).

She also works as a costume supervisor, prop and costume maker and education facilitator for theatres across the UK.

PABLO FERNANDEZ BAZ – LIGHTING DESIGNER

Recent Lighting Design credits: *El Medico, El Musical* (El tiempo entre costuras – Spain tour); *Warheads* (Oliver Award-nominated, Park Theatre); *Staged* (Winner Total Theatre awards for Circus 2019, Contemporary Circus production); *United Queendom* (site-specific, immersive production Kensington Palace, produced by Les Enfants Terribles); *Nearly Human* (Offie nominated, IDEA 2020, by Perhaps contraption); *Valhalla* (site-specific directed by Rich Rusk, nominated Offfest short run 2019).

Other companies Pablo has collaborated with include Talawa Theatre, The Sleeping Trees, Little Soldier Productions, Nofit Circus state.

DINAH MULLEN – SOUND DESIGNER

Dinah is a Bristol-based sound artist/designer for live and digital performance, specialising in dance, participatory work and devising. Dinah was a recipient of the Arts Council England Develop your Creative Practice award in 2021 and is currently developing work in the forms of sonic fiction and audio walks.

Trained: Rose Bruford.

Sound Design credits: *The Bolds* (The Unicorn Theatre); *Squirrel, Nora, Marie Antoinette, Antigone, The Waiting Room, The Changing Room, Dracula, Basset, Boudica, Aurora, Blank, The Hound of the Baskervilles* (The Egg, Theatre Royal Bath); *Who's Afraid of Virginia Woolf* (Tobacco Factory); *Homing Birds* (UK tour); *Bobby and Amy* (UK tour); *Your Sexts are Shit* (Touring); *D-DAY 75* (The Watermill/Newbury Corn Exchange); *Keith, The Plague, Richard III, The Daughter in Law, Insignificance,* (Arcola Theatre); *Sundowning* (UK tour); *The Droves* (CONEY); *Roller* (Barbican Pit); *Stella* (LIFT Festival/Brighton Theatre Royal/Holland Festival).

JENNIFER JACKSON – MOVEMENT DIRECTOR

Jennifer is a Latinx British-Bolivian theatre-maker, movement director and actor. She was awarded a Jerwood Live Work Fund for her work on TAKE SPACE (2021) and is a Bank Artist with Sheffield Theatres.

Theatre credits: *Kes* (Octagon Theatre Bolton); *The Merchant of Venice* (Shakespeare's Globe); *Five Children and It* (Theatre Royal Bath); *Endurance* (Home Manchester/BAC); *The Mountaintop, Cuttin' It, Wuthering Heights, Death of a Salesman, Queens of the Coal Age, Our Town* (Royal Exchange Theatre); *Baby Reindeer* (Francesca Moody Productions/The Bush – Olivier Award 2020); *Midnight Movie, Invisible Summer, Living Newspaper* (Royal Court Theatre); *Perspective* (New Views National Theatre); *Amsterdam* (ATC/Orange Tree/Theatre Royal Plymouth); *Pops* (Jake Orr Productions); *I Wanna Be Yours* (Paines Plough/Bush Theatre); *Parliament Square* (Bush Theatre/Royal Exchange Theatre); *The Strange Undoing of Prudencia Hart* (New Vic Theatre); *Be My Baby, Around the World in 80 Days* (Leeds Playhouse); *The Trick* (Bush Theatre/HighTide); *Philoxenia* (Bush Theatre); *Mountaintop* - UK tour (Young Vic/Desara Productions Ltd); *Mayfly, Out of Water* (Orange Tree); *Brighton Rock* (Pilot Theatre/The Lowry); *Island Town, Sticks and Stones, How to Spot an Alien* (Paines Plough Roundabout); *Black Mountain, How to be a Kid, Out of Love* (Paines Plough & Orange Tree); *The Ugly One* (The Park).

Events include: *Coventry Moves* for Coventry City of Culture 2021.

KAITLIN HOWARD – FIGHT DIRECTOR

Kaitlin qualified as a Stage Combat instructor in 2005, she is a teaching and examining member of The Academy of Performance Combat and is one of only three women on the Equity Register of Fight Directors.

Fight Direction credits: *Red Ellen* (Northern Stage/Nottingham Playhouse/ Edinburgh Lyceum); *The Scent of Roses, Life Is a Dream* (Edinburgh Lyceum); *Guards at the Taj* (Theatre By The Lake, Keswick); *A Midsummer Night's Dream, Our Country's Good* (The Tobacco Factory, Bristol); *The Jungle Book, A Skull In Connemara, Jack & The Beanstalk, Aladdin* (Oldham Coliseum); *The Merry Wives of Windsor* (Storyhouse, Chester); *The Little Mermaid, Cherry Jezebel* (Liverpool Everyman); *Hushabye Mountain, A Kidnapping, Orphans, The Trial, The Pride, Hamlet* (Hope Mill Theatre, Manchester); *Twelfth Night, The Illusion* (HOME, Manchester); *Robin Hood* (Cast, Doncaster); *Drych* (Theatr Genedlaethol Cymru); *Romeo and Juliet, Macbeth* (The Epstein Theatre, Liverpool); *The Comedy of Errors* (Greenwich Playhouse); *Killer Joe* (The Pleasance Theatre, London).

SARAH-JANE SCHOSTACK – ASSISTANT DIRECTOR

Trained: Theatre Studies at Ithaca College (US) and currently studying MFA Theatre Directing at Birkbeck, University of London.

Assistant Director credits: *The Last Five Years* (Garrick Theatre, West End); Taylor Mac's *The Fre* (The Flea, NYC); *Gone Too Far, Barbarians* (Guildhall School of Music and Drama); *The Trip to Bountiful* (Hangar Theatre, US); *The Stone Will Roll* (New York Theatre Workshop, NYC).

Directing credits: *Urinetown the Musical* (Lost Nation Theatre, US); *James and the Giant Peach* (Barrington Stage Company, US); *Singin in the Rain* (Ngau Chi Wan Civic Centre, Hong Kong); *Spring Awakening, Frozen Jr., Mamma Mia* (John W. Engeman Theatre, US); *Junie B Jones the Musical* (Cider Mill Playhouse, US); *It's a Wonderful Life* (Sheboygan Theatre Company, US); *What I Left Behind* (Hudson Theatre Guild, NYC); *The Stand-Ins* (Manhattan Repertory Theatre, NYC); *boom* (The Bridge at Shetler, NYC); *The Somewhat True Tale of Robin Hood* (New London Barn Playhouse, US).

JACK BOISSIEUX – PRODUCTION MANAGER

Jack is a freelance production manager, working across theatre, musicals, events and opera.

Recent Production Management credits: *The Choir of Man* (Arts Theatre, London & US tour), *Waterperry Opera Festival*, National Youth Theatre's *Annual Fundraising Gala*.

LISA COCHRANE – COMPANY STAGE MANAGER

Lisa is a freelance stage manager based in London. Originally from Northern Ireland, Lisa found her way across the Irish Sea and completed her drama school training in Professional Production Skills at Guildford School of Acting.

Lisa has previously worked with TFP on *Honour* (Park Theatre); *Disco Pigs* (Trafalgar Studios); *The Acedian Pirates* (Theatre503); *All Our Children* (Jermyn Street); *Land of Our Fathers* (Trafalgar Studios/national tour).

As Company Stage Manager on Book: Olivier Nominated – *Songs for Nobodies* (Ambassadors Theatre); *The Hunting of the Snark* (Queen Elizabeth Hall).

As Stage Manager on Book: *This Beautiful Future, For Services Rendered, Miss Julie, Creditors, Tonight at 8.30* (Jermyn Street Theatre).

As Deputy Stage Manager: *Hamlet* (Guildford Shakespeare); *Peter Pan*, *Dick Whittington*, *Snow White* (Swan Theatre, High Wycombe); *The Offing* (SJT & Live Theatre Newcastle); *King Lear* (The Grange Festival); *Vienna '34 – Munich '38* (Theatre Royal Bath); *The Hunting of the Snark* (Vaudeville Theatre).

CAITLIN CHATFIELD – ASSISTANT STAGE MANAGER

As Assistant Stage Manager: *Aladdin* (CAST Theatre); *Saturnalia* (Contact Youth Company/Level Up/High Rise Theatre); *Am-Dram, The Musical Comedy* (Quick Fantastic); *Cinderella* (CAST Theatre); *BD Stories* (Freedom Studios); *Maggie the Cat* (MIF – Manchester and Hamburg); *Beauty and the Beast* (UK Productions); *Rachel Tucker: Unplugged* (Pleasance Courtyard, Edinburgh).

As Stage Manager: *Bad Roads* (ALRA North); *How to Be A Better Human* (Brave Words Theatre Company); *Aleiah's Adventure* (R&D at Z-Arts); *Parallels – Signal Fires* (Yellow Earth Theatre Company); *Hidden* (Manchester Camerata); *WAPA Showcase* (Wirral Academy of Performing Arts); *Rush* (The King's Head Theatre); *Co:Lab Festival* (Royal Exchange Theatre); *The Egoist* (53two); *Bradford Literature Festival*.

Further credits: AV Design, *How to Be A Better Human* (Brave Words Theatre Company); Lighting Designer, *Rush* (The King's Head Theatre); Follow Spot Operator, *Rachel Tucker* (Shoreditch Town Hall); Rehearsal Stage Manager, *Dracula* (Creation Theatre Company); Venue Manager, *Ace Dome* (Pleasance Edinburgh Fringe); Props Assistant, *Hushabye Mountain* (Hope Mill Theatre); Show Caller, *Our City, Our Festival* (MIF).

NIPARUN NESSA – COMMUNITY ENGAGEMENT OFFICER

Niparun Nessa is a teacher, freelance arts facilitator and the community engagement officer at the Octagon Theatre. Niparun teaches at a secondary school and runs her own creative and aerial arts classes and workshops. Niparun has been looking at diversity in the arts and is working for the Octagon Theatre to network and make connections with diverse communities in and around Bolton and encourage everyone to access the shows and facilities the theatre has to offer.

Tara Finney Productions (TFP) is an award-winning, independent theatre production company, founded in 2013. TFP focuses on producing new writing, in the UK and internationally.

TFP's 20th anniversary production of Enda Walsh's *Disco Pigs* starring Evanna Lynch (*Harry Potter*) transferred to the Irish Repertory Theatre, New York, garnering a Critics' Pick from the New York Times. In 2019, TFP's co-production of *good dog* by Olivier Award-nominated writer Arinzé Kene completed its second tour of the UK and *Build a Rocket* was a Best Theatre Weekly Award winner at the Adelaide Fringe before touring the UK in autumn 2019. In the following summer, TFP was associate producer on the world premiere of Oscar nominated writer Anthony McCarten's (*The Two Popes, Darkest Hour, The Theory of Everything*) new play *The Pope* at Royal & Derngate, Northampton, starring Anton Lesser (*Game of Thrones, The Crown*). In late spring 2021, TFP's production of *The Greatest Play in the History of the World…* starring Julie Hesmondhalgh (*Broadchurch, Coronation Street*), re-opened theatres across the north of England with a UK tour.

Productions include: *The Greatest Play in the History of the World…* (UK tour, Trafalgar Studios, Royal Exchange Theatre, Traverse Theatre: The Stage Edinburgh Award Winner), *seeds* (UK tour), *Build a Rocket* (UK tour, Adelaide Fringe, Edinburgh Fringe, Latitude Festival: The Stage Best New Play of the Year), *The Pope* (Royal & Derngate), *good dog* (UK tour 2017 & 2019), *Disco Pigs* (Irish Repertory Theatre, New York, Trafalgar Studios: Origins 1st Irish Festival Award Winner, New York Times Critics' Pick), *Burkas and Bacon Butties* (VAULT Festival), *All Our Children* (Jermyn Street Theatre), *The Acedian Pirates, WINK* (Theatre503), *And Then Come The Nightjars* (UK tour), *Land of Our Fathers* (BBC Arts Online, Found111, UK tour, Trafalgar Studios, Theatre503: Time Out Fringe Show of the Year).

TFP's productions have been nominated for in excess of twenty-five awards including OffWestEnd Awards, UK Theatre Awards, the Susan Smith Blackburn Award and the Chita Rivera Awards, New York.

tarafinney.com
twitter.com/tara_finney
instagram.com/tara_finneyinsta
facebook.com/tarafinneyproductions

THEATRE. MADE IN BOLTON.

The Octagon is a producing theatre situated at the heart of Bolton. We are bold, adventurous and popular, making theatre of the highest quality, and a brilliant creative home for the people of Bolton and beyond. Our ambition is to be vital to a healthier and happier community.

The Octagon is an artistic hub, producing new and accessible art for all. We create theatre in the belief that this can enrich communities and fundamentally change people's lives for the better. Our engagement programmes provide creative opportunities for all ages. We believe that everyone has their own story and that theatre can be an amazing tool in empowering and building the confidence of people to tell these stories.

The Octagon was officially opened on 27 November 1967 by HRH Princess Margaret; it was the first theatre to be built in the North West since World War Two. In 2018, the theatre underwent a major redevelopment. Following the 2020 global pandemic, the theatre finally reopened its door to the public in May 2021. The new Octagon has seen a complete modernisation of the entire building, with updated performance spaces and an improved front of house experience. It is now fit for generations to come.

We are absolutely delighted to be working with Tara Finney Productions in staging the World Premiere of *Habibti Driver* by Shamia Chalabi and Sarah Henley in Bolton.

Chief Executive: Roddy Gauld
Artistic Director: Lotte Wakeham

The Octagon Theatre is a Registered Charity No. 248833

octagonbolton.co.uk
twitter.com/octagontheatre
Instagram.com/octagontheatre
facebook.com/OctagonBolton

HABIBTI DRIVER

Shamia Chalabi and Sarah Henley

Dedicated to Benjamin James Turner.
Supporter of theatre, lover of the arts
and always a champion of his friends.
Your book ran out of pages far too soon,
so this one is dedicated to you.

Characters

YUSUF
ASHRAF
SHAZIA
CHRIS
JEAN
YASMIN

Note on Text

A forward slash (/) indicates an interruption.

This text went to press before the end of rehearsals and so may differ slightly from the play as performed.

Scene One

We see an empty cab with the hazard lights on, Arabic music blaring out. There are fragrance trees hanging off the mirror along with some '99 names of Allah' prayer beads. There's a plastic bag with Arabic writing on it on the passenger seat and a few empty mugs littered around the cab. The radio crackles.

YUSUF. Driver 1154, can I have your location?

Pause.

1154 please come in, can I have your location?

Pause.

ASHRAF, COME IN, MAN! I've got a job for you!

ASHRAF *rushes back to the car, hands full with coffee, a pie, some Hula Hoops and a cigarette. He spills the coffee on himself as he gets into the car and presses the receiver.*

ASHRAF. Shit! Shit! Yes I'm here!

YUSUF. You can't be taking these liberties! Let me guess, picking up snacks?

ASHRAF. No, no, nothing like that.

YUSUF. Coffee then?

ASHRAF. Excuse me but I am professional – no stopping while working, brother, okay? You still on that diet?

YUSUF. You know Hafifah – she's tap-tap-tap in my head – lose weight, stop smoking, this, that. But Alhamdulillah I feel good! You should try it too!

ASHRAF. Yusuf, I have already a wife and a daughter – there is no more space for a nagging-horse brother –

YUSUF. I'm right though – you'll be getting the diabetes soon… you should be thanking me for the reminder –

ASHRAF. Thanking you?! Oh yes! Big welcome home, Ashraf, isn't it? 'No snack breaks'... 'diabetes knock knocking on your door'... anything else? Am I breathing too loudly? Want me to iron my underpants some more? As my loving brother, you should be asking me how Egypt was.

Pause.

YUSUF. How was Egypt?

ASHRAF *relaxes into the conversation, putting a single Hula Hoop on each forkful of pie and then adding some of his 'special sauce' from a bottle in the cup holder.*

ASHRAF. Fantastic, man, good food, relaxation – no stress.

YUSUF. And Mama?

ASHRAF. You know, relieved...

YUSUF. Of course! Yasmin! Finally. Look – after shift come to the café with us? We go have some tea, talk –

ASHRAF. Sounds good – what time? I'm picking Shazia up.

A beat.

YUSUF. I saw Shazia in Makinson's Arcade the other day. Brother – when's she gonna start –

ASHRAF. I'm working on it.

YUSUF. She was with someone – a man.

ASHRAF. Probably a work colleague.

YUSUF. She was holding his hand. (*A beat.*) You should talk to her, get her to –

ASHRAF. I am, I am.

YUSUF. For the community, Ashraf – we can't have this. You can't allow it.

ASHRAF. Anyway – didn't you say there was a job?

YUSUF. Shit! The pick-up – I forgot – Millstone at the top of Wigan Lane –

ASHRAF *takes another forkful of pie with a Hula Hoop on it and crunches down.*

ASHRAF. On my way!

YUSUF. You *are* eating!

ASHRAF. Outrageous!

YUSUF. I can see your location. You're at Galloways?!

ASHRAF. You got me! The best pies in Wigan –

YUSUF. Aah –

ASHRAF. – spiced it up with some of my special sauce!

YUSUF. Bring me one, brother?

ASHRAF. Sorry… it's impossible.

YUSUF. Why?

ASHRAF. Your wife would kill me.

ASHRAF *hits the button to hang up the radio.*

YUSUF. Fine… but remember Shazia, okay, brother… brother?

Scene Two

Later that day. ASHRAF *is waiting in the car, smoking. He's slicking down what little hair he has with a brush, checking his teeth – trying to floss with a taxi receipt. He puts out the cigarette and tries to waft the smoke out. He then sprays some Joop from his bag of duty-free around the car.*

SHAZIA *arrives and takes her engagement ring off, moving it to another finger. She opens the door to get in and* ASHRAF *moves the plastic bag on the seat to his lap.*

ASHRAF. Hello, baby! Just some shells there – sorry. What, no hug?

He tries to hug her but she's rigid.

Shaz –

SHAZIA. You said you'd be gone a month.

I thought something had happened.

ASHRAF. Like what? I got stuck in the pyramids? I became a mummy? Got eaten by a camel?

SHAZIA. Not funny.

Didn't you even want to know how I was?

ASHRAF. Habibti – it was busy, and…

SHAZIA. Right.

Pause.

I was really worried –

ASHRAF. I brought you a present.

He passes her the bag with Arabic writing on.

SHAZIA. You think you can buy forgiveness, is that it? Is it jewellery?

ASHRAF. I'm a taxi driver – not a millionaire!

SHAZIA. Or perfume? I see you bought yourself some Joop. Nuts?!

ASHRAF. Special five-star gold-standard the best of bee's knees Egyptian nuts –

SHAZIA. Wait… that you've clearly opened and started eating!

ASHRAF. I got a bit hungry… it's the thought that counts, habibti!

SHAZIA. Thanks.

ASHRAF. In Arabic?

SHAZIA. Shukran.

*ASHRAF turns the radio on. Whitney Houston, 'I Wanna
Dance with Somebody' plays. ASHRAF sings and SHAZIA
joins in. The radio starts to crackle and YUSUF's voice can
be heard talking to another driver. ASHRAF switches the
taxi radio off and turns Whitney down.*

Dad... I need to tell you something and –

ASHRAF. Yusuf saw you the other day.

SHAZIA. Where? I didn't see him – why didn't he say hi?

ASHRAF. In Makinson's Arcade... he said you were with a
man – holding hands.

SHAZIA. Oh.

Silence.

ASHRAF. Have you thought about the headscarf thing? Please.
For me, habibti.

*A beat. ASHRAF fumbles around in his door and pulls out
a piece of paper, he hands it to SHAZIA.*

SHAZIA (*reading*). Spicy sauce name ideas: 'Sauce and Spice
and All Things Nice', 'Kiss My Sauce', 'Wigan Spice',
'Ashraf's Special Sauce'.

ASHRAF. It's good innit?

SHAZIA. You definitely can't use the last one.

ASHRAF. Why? It does what it says on the tin? If Birdseye
Captain can sell his fishy fingers then I can have my special
sauce.

SHAZIA. Fish fingers.

ASHRAF. I've been working on some new flavours, and it's
'mwaah'. I'm going to speak to Tony at the market...
Mr Nando had to start somewhere innit?

SHAZIA. Yep!

They listen to the radio for a few beats.

Dad – I've got something to tell you –

ASHRAF. So you'll think about the headscarf thing though, yes?

She reaches into the plastic bag to get some nuts.

SHAZIA. How's quitting smoking going?

ASHRAF. Good. I'm feeling good. Alhamdulillah!

SHAZIA. So what's this?

She presents a pack of duty-free cigarettes to him.

Spraying Joop everywhere doesn't mean I can't smell it.

ASHRAF *takes the cigarettes off her and leans across to put them in the glovebox. As he opens it a pack of pictures falls out and* SHAZIA *picks them up.*

ASHRAF. Leave them. I'll get them!

SHAZIA *looks through the pictures.*

SHAZIA. What? This is a… you're married?

ASHRAF. No, no, I'm not. I'm… engaged! This is a typical Egyptian engagement.

SHAZIA. Barely worth mentioning.

ASHRAF. Don't be sarcastic.

SHAZIA. How do you want me to be?

ASHRAF. Happy? Or silent.

Silence.

Look – I didn't go there to get… engaged, but it was your grandmother. She kept on saying I needed someone to take care of me, being divorced was no good. I didn't really want to but she introduced me, made me go along and –

SHAZIA. And forced you to get engaged? Yeah, I mean you look miserable, so unhappy… poor thing!

SHAZIA *picks up a picture and looks closely.*

I mean, her dress, all the guests – you're married, aren't you.

ASHRAF. Yes.

SHAZIA. You didn't think to invite me.

There's a moment of quiet.

ASHRAF. I'm lonely. You're busy – you have your own life, your boyfriend – which I could say a lot more about but… it's just me here. I get back from work and it's just me. I wake up all alone. I spend the day with strangers. I need somebody… to talk about the day with. And she's nice. She's got a good heart –

SHAZIA. Pretty.

ASHRAF. Yes but more than that – we laugh.

SHAZIA. How old is she?

ASHRAF. My age.

SHAZIA. Dad?!

ASHRAF. Okay… a bit younger.

SHAZIA. DAD?!

ASHRAF. Okay, okay, she's thirty-nine.

SHAZIA. Is she coming here?

ASHRAF. Soon. She's applying for the papers.

SHAZIA. You're her ticket.

ASHRAF. She's not like that – she's educated, a professor in a school. She's willing to come here and leave that for me. You'll like her. Trust me.

SHAZIA. I just don't think you've thought this through.

Silence.

Does Mum know?

Silence.

Does she speak English?

Silence.

How will you even support her?

ASHRAF. She will get allowance from me.

SHAZIA. Knew it.

ASHRAF. And when my sauce takes off she will work in the family business.

SHAZIA. Great. When *Dragon's Den* come knocking, yeah?

ASHRAF. We don't need this Peter Jones bastard. You can have job too, Shazia – there's plenty to go round.

SHAZIA. I've got a job, Dad! Flogging a few bottles of peri peri on Wigan market isn't going to cut it. Does she want kids?

ASHRAF. Enough. I've got a headache. Let's talk about this another time –

SHAZIA. Yep. Just drop me off at mine.

ASHRAF. And it's not peri peri.

Scene Three

SHAZIA *and* CHRIS *are setting up at a car-boot sale in Wigan. On one side of the boot is coins, stamps, pogs and football cards and the other is clothes and jewellery. They survey their boot.*

SHAZIA. Do you think it's all a bit niche?

CHRIS. What?

SHAZIA. Well, like… do you really think there's going to be a buyer for your Commonwealth stamp book?

CHRIS. That's my grandad's. He's dead.

SHAZIA. Or your Charles and Lady Di commemorative coin collection – I mean, why've you got five of them?

CHRIS. That was gonna be my pension. I'm telling you – when it all comes out that our Regina herself ordered the hit – those Natwest coins are gonna skyrocket –

SHAZIA. And who wants an N64 when you've got a Playstation 4? Let's face it no one's gonna pay for this stuff, why don't we just chuck it?

CHRIS. I'm not chucking it, Shaz. Nostalgia, memories, it's worth something. If I can get a hundred pound for that N64 then I'll let it go... for you. You're making me do this.

SHAZIA. We've got too much stuff. We can't start our life together with a flat full of junk!

CHRIS. Junk my arse – this is my life.

SHAZIA. Freaks me out is all I'm saying... don't serial killers collect things? Jesus... you're going to kill me in your sleep, aren't you –

CHRIS. Just stop.

SHAZIA. Okay. Sorry!

A beat.

CHRIS. I need a 'gimme'. I'm not ready. It's too much.

SHAZIA. What?

CHRIS. Let's both keep one thing. Just one.

SHAZIA. Fine. What. Which piece of crap do you want to keep so badly we have to have it cluttering up our marital home?

Pause.

Come on! They're walking past – we're losing potential customers here.

CHRIS. Fuck I don't know.

SHAZIA. Well, it can't be that important then, can it?

CHRIS. It's all bloody important, Shaz, okay? I think I'm having a breakdown! Fuck. Go on – you go first, I'm still thinking.

SHAZIA *looks at the items. She sees a scarf amongst some clothes and goes to pop it in her bag.*

That? Is that even yours? Looks like something my nan
would wear at the bus stop!

*He snatches it off her and puts it on his head doing an
impression of a bumbling old lady.*

Been waiting long, love?

SHAZIA. Chris. Stop.

CHRIS. Sorry – I've just never seen you in it is all – show me
it on!

*She considers it for a minute and then puts it on as a
headscarf.*

Christ – you look like a mad mullah!

SHAZIA. Course I do – you're bloody marrying one, knob'ead.

CHRIS. Give over, am I! I'm marrying Miss Deanery High
2008 if I remember correctly. What was that poem you did
for the talent bit… Wordsworth, weren't it – 'I wandered
lonely as a clou– '

SHAZIA. Fuck off!! What are you keeping then, Ian bloody
Brady?

CHRIS. Pogs. Has to be. I've got an off-centre one in there –
that's rare, and a No Fear one which was my favourite. I'm
not letting them go and that's that.

SHAZIA. Fine, you weirdo. Now, let's get on with it.

CHRIS. Can I keep my stamps too?

SHAZIA. You know marriage is all about compromise, right?
This does not bode well.

CHRIS. Compromise? What's that song you sing to me when
you nick my hoodies?

SHAZIA (*singing – to Whitney Houston's 'My Love is Your
Love'*). YOUR STUFF IS MY STUFF, AND MY STUFF IS
MY STUFF! You wouldn't fit in my hoodies anyway.

CHRIS. Okay. Fine. I suppose you're giving up a fair bit too.

SHAZIA. Not really. Like what? S'only clothes here.

CHRIS. Like… well… your name for a start?

SHAZIA. Who says?

CHRIS. Who says?

SHAZIA. Who says I'm giving up my name?

CHRIS. I bloody say, stupid! You're marrying me, aren't you?
Shazia Nadia Green – got a nice friendly ring to it, don't you
think?

SHAZIA. Well… I… I hadn't thought about it… I'm not sure
I –

CHRIS. Shaz… come on – that's the deal – I spend a small
fortune on a diamond, and you take my name – that's just
how it rolls –

SHAZIA. Fucking hell, Chris – I love it but it's from fucking
H Samuel's – you've not bloody paid for naming rights –
I'm an independent woman, not a prize fucking cow you've
just bought down the market – what… what about my
family?

CHRIS. Our Jean? She loves me!

SHAZIA. No! My dad! He's not gonna want me to be called
Mrs bloody Green is he?!

CHRIS. Why the fuck not?

SHAZIA. Just… just let me think about it, okay – it's, it's a bit
of a shock is all.

CHRIS. It's pretty normal practice, Shaz, yeah – shouldn't
really be that shocking. When are you going to tell him by
the way? Before or after the wedding?

SHAZIA. Chris, please – you don't get it –

CHRIS. Am I that embarrassing? Does my pog fetish shame
you that much? Or is it just –

SHAZIA. Please. It's complicated, okay. I'll tell him. I'm sorry.

CHRIS. Right.

SHAZIA. Keep the stamps as well. Keep it all –

CHRIS. I bloody will.

(*Packing up the pogs*.) And I don't need your permission anyway. And I'm having a chippy tea – this stupid wedding diet can do one.

SHAZIA. Whatever.

Scene Four

ASHRAF *is watching a video on his phone of a goat turning a tap on, chuckling to himself.* JEAN *climbs into the car – flustered, carrying many Lidl and B&M bags.*

JEAN. I hear congratulations are in order?

ASHRAF. What?

JEAN. Your new wife! Congratulations.

ASHRAF. Yes… well, it has been fifteen years, Jean –

JEAN. And don't I know it – you put me off men for life! Anyway, all the bloody best t'ya is all I say.

Pause.

Shazia seemed a bit, well… shocked. Was it, you know… arranged? She did know who she was getting, right?

ASHRAF. Course she bloody did! It is… how you say – one woman's trash is another woman's treasure.

(*Remembering to be offended*.) Anyway… this mithering is very rude!

JEAN. Well, look. Tell her to call me. You know, if she needs any advice.

ASHRAF. Oh yes, I'll be sure to give my new wife the direct line to my ex-wife, is Skypes okay or do you prefer Whatisapps?

JEAN. I'm being serious. And next time you go bloody galavanting just give Shaz a call or something, we were worried sick.

ASHRAF. Yes, I know. She already had a go –

JEAN. Oh, and I picked up some fancy bottles for you from Lidl's, you'll have to buy your own labels but they were on offer, honestly you should get down there – four ninety-nine for twelve –

ASHRAF *takes a call on speaker.*

ASHRAF. As-salaam alaikum, brother!

YUSUF. You see the game, brother?

ASHRAF. I'm working innit! I heard it though – sounded like it was quite a goal from Salah.

YUSUF. Ashraf, it was poetry – he stuck it BANG in the onion bag! Like the time I thrashed you in '89 at Aunt Fatima's… you cried like baby goat –

ASHRAF. You kicked me in the goonies, I had no shoes on *and* it was offside!

YUSUF. As they say – all is fair in love and football –

ASHRAF. Celebrations later?

YUSUF. Of course – come to the café! I've put you on for double shifts next week okay?

ASHRAF. Which days? I have some meetings, Inshallah.

YUSUF. I told you this stupid sauce won't pay your bills. You want Yasmin to think you're foolish?

JEAN *tuts loudly.*

Did you speak to Shazia?

ASHRAF. Yes yes – it's all sorted.

JEAN. What's / sorted?

ASHRAF. She'll be... erm... covered when you next see her, don't you worry.

YUSUF. And the man?

ASHRAF *starts coughing to cover what* JEAN *says next*.

JEAN. She bloody well won't be – over my dead / body.

ASHRAF. Just a colleague.

YUSUF. Is Jean there?

ASHRAF. No... of course not – why?

YUSUF. Oh nothing... I just thought I heard that familiar huffing and grunting – is it diabetes do you think? All those roasts yes – very crispy Yorkshire puddings and the gravy –

ASHRAF. Nope, and nope. She's strong like a... bull.

JEAN. Bloody cheek.

ASHRAF. Shhhh.

YUSUF. Ashraf.

ASHRAF. What?

YUSUF. Never mind the grunting like pig – I can see your location – you're at Gala Bingo!

ASHRAF. It's two buses, Yusuf, she's Shazia's mother and the 311 is never on time – just leave it, okay?

YUSUF. Fine, fine... but tell her if she wins the big bingo bonus she has to pay for once. Her days are numbered for all this anyway.

ASHRAF. What?

YUSUF. Yasmin!

ASHRAF. Right –

YUSUF. Pick-up in Aspull, okay – I'm sending details through now.

ASHRAF. Fine.

ASHRAF *hangs up the phone*.

JEAN. Some things never bloody change.

ASHRAF. And some things do.

JEAN. Yep. You've finally got the good Egyptian wife you've always wanted.

ASHRAF. That's not fair.

JEAN. Right. Well, it wouldn't hurt to drag a bastard hoover round this car before she gets here.

Scene Five

CHRIS *is driving and* SHAZIA *is in the passenger seat. They've just been for their regular date night – 'Groupon Tuesdays' which was her choice this week – life drawing.* SHAZIA *is holding both of their drawings.*

SHAZIA. Groupon Tuesdays – bargain, mate! Twelve ninety-nine for the two of us.

CHRIS. I can think of better ways to spend an hour and a half that don't involve staring at wrinkly old Rodger's todger.

SHAZIA. Leave off – you loved it! Anyway, this is the start of us being more 'cultured' – just try.

CHRIS. What – hanging out with a load of old fogies at Wigan Life Centre? Shaz, there are some things you can't un-see.

SHAZIA (*ignoring him and continuing to be cultured*). I had no idea you were so good with the charcoal –

CHRIS (*joining her*). I did an art GCSE –

SHAZIA. I can tell –

CHRIS. Yeah – I really got into it, you know, like a sort of healthy… flow state –

SHAZIA. He certainly looks healthy here – I mean, the shading on his ball sack – impressive, almost like you've been practising –

CHRIS. Yes, I think it's safe to agree, the scrotum is perfection.

SHAZIA. Will you love me when I'm that old and wrinkly?

CHRIS. No chance – I've seen your mum – I reckon you'll hit your prime at around thirty-eight and then I'm off.

SHAZIA. Oi!

CHRIS. Nah, course I will – but you need to start moisturising your neck – it often gets neglected in one's day-to-day regime – I read that in *Bella* at the dentist's.

SHAZIA. No problem – as long as you keep on top of those ear pubes – they're gross.

CHRIS. Too far. You know I'm worried about that – you've seen my Uncle Gary.

SHAZIA. You think that's bad – you should see my Aunt Hafifah – so thick I can't believe she hasn't gone deaf with it!

A beat.

CHRIS. I'd love to see your Aunt Hafifah's ear hair, but you won't let me.

SHAZIA (*ignoring*). Your turn to book the next date night – got to be cultured, mind. I think I set the bar pretty high if I do say so myself –

CHRIS (*letting her*). They've got a clay cock casting class in the geriatric ward at the Wigan Infirmary on a Wednesday –

SHAZIA. Stop it, you're making me hungry. Shall we pick up some tea – what do you fancy?

CHRIS. Something exotic?

SHAZIA. Iceland do a good crispy duck.

CHRIS. Nah, fajitas.

SHAZIA. That's not exotic!

CHRIS. Fajitas and sex?

SHAZIA. Only if you draw me like you did your grandad tonight – I bet he does a good crispy f–

CHRIS (*laughing*). No! You're a wrong un. I bloody love you.

Pause.

SHAZIA. I'm meeting my dad's new wife tomorrow.

CHRIS. Jesus – you kept that quiet. Want me to come?

SHAZIA. No.

CHRIS. Course. (*A beat.*) You've still not told him, have you?

SHAZIA. Just shut up about it okay?

A beat.

CHRIS. I didn't want to do this.

SHAZIA. What?

CHRIS. Right, here goes. If you don't tell him. This week. Well. Well, the wedding's off.

SHAZIA. You're threatening me.

CHRIS. I've tried being patient, Shaz, don't make me the bad guy here.

SHAZIA. God forbid.

CHRIS. He got married without telling you. He's not got a leg to stand on… just bloody tell him.

SHAZIA. Or we call it a day.

CHRIS. I obviously don't want to do that –

SHAZIA. But that's what you're saying.

CHRIS. Yep. Yeah it is.

Scene Six

ASHRAF *and* SHAZIA *are at the airport.*

ASHRAF. Where's your headscarf?

SHAZIA. I told you, she can meet me how I am.

ASHRAF. Here, put this on.

> ASHRAF *takes off a woolly tartan scarf.* SHAZIA *doesn't take it.*

Don't embarrass me –

SHAZIA. Just calm down.

ASHRAF. You calm down!

> *He slicks down his remaining hair.*

Pass me a chewing gum.

> *She reaches into the glovebox and gets it out.*

SHAZIA. Normal, or Juicy Fruit.

ASHRAF. Normal. Pass me Joop.

> SHAZIA *gets it out and passes it over and* ASHRAF *begins spraying.*

SHAZIA. Go easy!

ASHRAF. Arab women like it. Look – you think I've lost weight?

SHAZIA. Since when?!

ASHRAF. I've lost weight, isn't it? Look I have – see?

SHAZIA. Yes, Dad. You lost weight. You look great.

ASHRAF. Good. Thank you.

> ASHRAF *checks his watch.*

Five minutes.

SHAZIA. Dad, there was something I wanted to say the other day, something I need to tell you –

ASHRAF. You'll like her, habibti. Trust me –

SHAZIA. Before she arrives we should talk about a few
things –

ASHRAF. You will always be my habibti, my number one –

His phone beeps.

Where's the flowers?

SHAZIA *passes them to him.*

Okay. I'll be five minutes. Please, Shazia, just be…
respectful.

SHAZIA *takes the price tag off of the flowers and gives him
a kiss.*

SHAZIA. Just… before you go, there's something you should
know –

ASHRAF. Hurry up and wish me luck, Shazia!

SHAZIA. Good luck.

ASHRAF. Thank you.

ASHRAF *leaves to get* YASMIN.

SHAZIA (*a huge sigh*). Fuck.

SHAZIA *picks up her dad's scarf and puts it on. She looks at
herself for a minute then freaks out and takes it off.*

ASHRAF *returns with* YASMIN. SHAZIA *gets out of the
car to greet her.*

ASHRAF. Shazia, this is Yasmin. (*To* YASMIN.) Binti, Shazia.
[*My daughter Shazia.*]

YASMIN (*to* ASHRAF). Dee helwa awi. [*She is very pretty.*]

ASHRAF. She says you get your good looks from me.

YASMIN *goes to embrace* SHAZIA. *She kisses both her
cheeks and speaks in broken English.*

YASMIN. Very nice to meet you.

SHAZIA. Thank you!

(*Shouting slowly.*) YOUR ENGLISH IS GOOD!

ASHRAF. She's not deaf, Shazia.

SHAZIA. So… good flight?

YASMIN. Pardon?

SHAZIA (*louder with a thumbs up and an aeroplane signal*).
Good flight?

YASMIN. Ah, aywa, shokran. El mawazafeen Kano lotaaf, el
ekl kan momtaz, wa wasalna fe wa2t el kwayis-el wahid ayiz
ey aktar min kidda? [*Ah yes. Thank you. The staff were very
friendly, the food was excellent and we landed on time –
what more could you want!*]

ASHRAF (*translating*). Yes.

Silence.

SHAZIA. Who did you fly with?

ASHRAF. Ay khat tayaran? [*Which airline?*]

YASMIN. Leh bitisaalni el soaall dah? Fee hagat ahem min
kidda. Mish ihna Lissa mitgawizeen? [*Why is she asking me
this? There are more important things? We've just got
married!*]

ASHRAF. Hat titaalimi, fi engiltirra be oulo aleyha 'small talk'.
Inti mahzooza inimatkalimitkeesh aan el gaw. [*In England
they call it 'small-talk' – you will learn. You're lucky she's
not talking about the weather!*]

YASMIN. KLM.

SHAZIA. Aah – every time I've flown with them they've been
bloody late!

ASHRAF. Shazia, language!

SHAZIA. What is the weather like in Egypt?

ASHRAF. Hot.

SHAZIA. I was asking Yasmin!

ASHRAF. El ghasala bita3it-ha bazit. [*Her washing machine broke*.] Khadit el tora7 lil maghsala. [*She took her hijabs to the cleaner*.] Kol 7aga itsaraait. [*Everything got stolen*.]

SHAZIA. Dad. What are you saying? I know you're talking about me! Dad – ENGLISH!

YASMIN. I'm sorry to hear. Not good.

SHAZIA. About what?

ASHRAF. I was telling her what happened to your headscarves.

SHAZIA. Oh yeah?

ASHRAF. Yeah – you know that your washing machine broke, so you took them to the laundrette and someone stole all of your washing.

SHAZIA. Ah yeah. All of it. Gone. Bastards!

ASHRAF. Shazia – language.

YASMIN. Ana aandi torrah kiteera, momkin adeeki law ayza. [*I have many headscarves – I can give you some if you like?*]

ASHRAF. She said that you should be covered up, and she's happy to borrow you some headscarves.

SHAZIA. Thank you.

ASHRAF. In Arabic.

SHAZIA. Er, Shukran, Yasmin.

YASMIN. You have dinner today?

SHAZIA. Oh no, I can't, I have to meet my boyfriend.

YASMIN. You have boyfriend?

(*To* ASHRAF.) Ya Ashraf ma oltileesh ley? [*Ashraf, why didn't you tell me?*]

(*To* SHAZIA.) He must come.

SHAZIA. Ah no. It's okay. He's at work till late but I said I would cook.

YASMIN. He is… new yes?

SHAZIA. No – four years.

YASMIN. Long time.

> (*To* ASHRAF.) Eh ma-abiltohoosh, kidda may sahish. Kidda Mish kwayis ya Ashraf. Lazim te eblo! [*Why haven't you met him, this is not good. This is terrible, Ashraf. You must meet this man!?*]

> (*To* SHAZIA.) Shazia, we all have meeting? Soon? Please – not good that Ashraf not met…?

SHAZIA. Chris.

YASMIN. Yes Chris. So yes we –

ASHRAF. Yasmin, no, they're very busy. I am busy with work –

YASMIN. Ashraf, ihna osra. Eyla. El awlawaya el eyla. [*Ashraf, it's family. Family. Family is number one.*] Shazia, you come to the house.

SHAZIA. Or we could go for a drink at The Star… bucks, on Wigan Lane. You know, have a latte or a frappe mochaccino – ever had one of those, Yasmin? They're great… or a muffin. But I won't have a muffin 'cause I don't really eat cake. And no er –

ASHRAF. Any place you like.

SHAZIA. Okay?

ASHRAF (*proudly*). This. Is my taxi.

Scene Seven

SHAZIA *and* JEAN *are in the car –* SHAZIA *in the front passenger seat,* JEAN *in the back.*

SHAZIA. This is why I need to pass my test. I can't be doing with this.

JEAN. What's he getting? I told him to sack off Asda's – Lidl is much cheaper –

SHAZIA. You heard – said he were 'nipping in' to get a lottery ticket and now we're just sat here like two dickheads. Bloody patriarchy this is.

JEAN. I did offer you lessons ten year ago.

SHAZIA. I know… just at that point the street-dancing lessons were more important… thought I were gonna be a Pussycat Doll, didn't I? That's the fucking patriarchy and all.

JEAN. Say patriarchy one more time and I'm off. You're like a broken record.

SHAZIA. Bloody hell! Sorry.

A beat.

JEAN. Seen your dad?

SHAZIA. No. Why'd you think Chris is driving me?

JEAN. Thought yous two would be thick as thieves now he's back.

SHAZIA. Yeah… well, me too. But he's got a new wife, hasn't he, so…

JEAN. Come on, she can't be that bad if she's putting up with Ashraf?

SHAZIA. I wouldn't know. She doesn't speak English – seems very 'devout' – she wants me covered up. And so does he.

JEAN. Right.

SHAZIA. And she gets a fucking allowance while I'm scrabbling like a knobhead at car-boot sales, selling practically everything we own to pay for my wedding.

JEAN. Well, did you tell him about the wedding?

SHAZIA. I bloody tried, okay! I TRIED! And I don't need any more pressure from you, or Chris, or bloody anyone. I *know* he needs to know. I *know* they need to meet. I *know* the wedding's off if I don't sort it. I KNOW. And I am bloody trying. Okay?

JEAN. Right.

SHAZIA. Sorry.

A beat.

Is it weird for you, like. That he's re-married.

JEAN. It's been a long time.

SHAZIA. I know. Yeah. Just he's gone for someone very –

JEAN. Different?

SHAZIA. Yeah... I guess... never mind.

A beat.

Do you feel sad, though? Like pushed out. Or. Are you ready to meet someone do you think? Or. Are you happy like? On your own?

JEAN. Bloody hell, what is this – *Oprah*?

SHAZIA. Sorry.

JEAN. No. S'okay. Fair question after fifteen years.

A beat.

SHAZIA. So?

JEAN. So. Your dad was the one for me, mental as that sounds. We just couldn't bridge the gap. Scrap that, we could, just everyone else couldn't.

SHAZIA. So that's it?

JEAN. I don't know. I've been satisfied like being friends. Course that might all change now... so maybe I'll need to have a look at it again.

SHAZIA. Yeah. Well, I'll be driving you soon. So if you need a lift to meet your date from SilverSingles or whatever, I'll be here.

JEAN. Oi, cheeky bugger – how old do you think I am?

SHAZIA. Sorry.

JEAN. S'okay.

A beat.

SHAZIA. Sometimes I think it'd be easier to just cut him out… you know. Be one thing. He's fucking shit anyway.

JEAN. No need… let him decide. You can't please everyone. You've just got to do you and let us all deal with it. You've got to tell him – it's gone on too long now.

SHAZIA. I know!

JEAN. Wanna ring Chris?

SHAZIA. There he is. Bloody hell – what's he got? We haven't got space for any more shite.

JEAN. Compromise, Shaz – he's a good'n and you know it. Looks like some sort of a paddling pool… it's an inflatable hot tub!

SHAZIA. Fuck's sake. We're not made o'money! Where does he think we are?

JEAN. Costa del Sol?

Scene Eight

ASHRAF *is in the driver's seat and* YASMIN *is in the passenger seat.* YASMIN *is leaning down and looking at* ASHRAF*'s feet.*

ASHRAF. Lesson one – clutch control. Watch! Watch – are you watching?

YASMIN. Yes.

ASHRAF. You see my right one goes down, and the left eases up. See?

YASMIN. Yes.

ASHRAF. So show me.

YASMIN. Asl mafeesh dawasat hena, mumkin – [*I don't have any pedals here. Can't I –*]

ASHRAF. In English.

YASMIN. No. Pedals.

ASHRAF. Just imagine you have pedals.

YASMIN. Imagine.

ASHRAF. Right.

YASMIN. Okay. So I push down –

ASHRAF. Smoothly. Smoothly! You can't be jerking like that!

YASMIN. It *is* smoothly. There's no pedals – how do you know if it's smoothly!

ASHRAF. I can see, okay – I have eyes!

YASMIN. You also have brain, but you still only drive taxi for living.

ASHRAF. At the moment – you wait until my business –

YASMIN. Your business this, your business that – how is it you say? More trousers, less talk, yes?

ASHRAF. Well, just you remember who is wearing the trousers here okay?

YASMIN. They will not fit very long if you keep with these pies… and chippy teas, babby's yed, party meat pies…

ASHRAF. Finished?

YASMIN. What is babby's yed anyway?

ASHRAF. Go again. Smoothly.

YASMIN. I do it on the pedals. Engine off.

ASHRAF. Fine.

They switch seats.

YASMIN. Like this?

ASHRAF. Yes. Keep going. Twenty times at least.

YASMIN. Right.

ASHRAF *gets some flashcards out of his pocket.*

ASHRAF. King Henry VIII's daughter Mary was a devout Catholic and persecuted Protestants, which is why she became known as: A) Catholic Mary, B) Killer Mary, C) Bloody Mary or D) There's Something About Mary.

YASMIN. She was Catholic. 'A' please. Catholic Mary.

ASHRAF. Yes.

(*Looking down and seeing he's wrong.*) No. Not good. Your English is coming but if you want to live here you must blend in. Mix and blend. Smoothly – smoothly!

YASMIN. Okay!

ASHRAF*'s phone rings – he picks up on speaker.*

YUSUF. Brother. Where are you?

ASHRAF. It's my day off, yes? I'm teaching Yasmin to drive!

YUSUF. In the taxi?

ASHRAF. Er… No – just theory.

YUSUF. Hey, you'll like this – what takes up twelve parking spaces?

ASHRAF. What?

YUSUF. Six women drivers!

ASHRAF. Classic.

YUSUF. Oh, and what's worse than a woman using your credit card?

ASHRAF. What?

YUSUF. A woman driving your car!

ASHRAF. Ha! Is this why Hafifah keeps on with that micro-scooter? Brother, she's so fast –

YUSUF. Trust me – Wigan is a safer place! Anyway – you were missed at mosque.

ASHRAF. Ah – sorry – catch you later for tea? Maybe some sheesha?

YUSUF. Yes! Will Shazia be coming later with Yasmin? Omar wants her to meet his son. Very good match.

ASHRAF. Apart from the eye –

YUSUF. Omar has assured me it's not genetic.

ASHRAF. I've told you before – no dowry, no Shazia.

YUSUF. Ah – you can't be putting a price on my favourite niece! Let them meet at least? Mosque next week?

ASHRAF. I'll ask her.

YUSUF. You tell her. Anyway, Hafifiah has some Mahshi for Yasmin – she will bring it. You get that video of the goat and the tap?

ASHRAF. Yes, brother! Such a good one! I have one of a goat squealing like a human that I will send you later.

YUSUF. Shukran.

ASHRAF. Right.

He hangs up the phone. Gets out another card.

Pubs are usually open from A) 8 a.m. –

YASMIN. How dare he speak of women in this way?

ASHRAF. B) 9 a.m. –

YASMIN. And what's this about Omar, Shazia has boyfriend already?

ASHRAF. C) 10 a.m. –

YASMIN. And I don't want Mahshi from Hafifah if it means listening to her gossip –

ASHRAF. Or D) 11 a.m.

YASMIN. And what are these stupid goats videos, eh?

ASHRAF. Concentrate! Pubs?

YASMIN. I don't believe in pubs.

ASHRAF. For the English, pubs is like mosque.

YASMIN. All this drinking is shameful.

ASHRAF. You must never say that in Wigan.

YASMIN. No wonder they end up with Killer Queen Mary – she was probably, how you say, rats arsed?

ASHRAF. Smoothly! Right, two more questions then you sing National Anthem.

YASMIN. And speaking of rats you also need to tell Yusuf to stick it where it's dark outside, yes?

Scene Nine

Late at night, SHAZIA *is drunk, standing on the side of the road, crying and mumbling as* ASHRAF *screeches in.*

ASHRAF. Get in. Get in before anybody sees! What time do you call this?

SHAZIA *sits on the kerb.* ASHRAF *reluctantly gets out.*

Where is your coat? It's bloody freezing!

SHAZIA. S'over.

ASHRAF. What are you saying? Speak English. Are you drunk?

SHAZIA (*thinking for a minute*). Yes.

ASHRAF. Eeb aleeki, Shazia. [*Shame on you, Shazia.*]

Silence.

Were you spiked?

SHAZIA. No.

ASHRAF. So this is it? You're drinking alcohol now?

Silence.

Shazia?

Silence.

Shazia, be honest with me. I am your father. Respect at all times. Are you drinking alcohol now?

SHAZIA (*snapping*). Aaargh! YES! Well not *now*, exactly... been getting wasted most weekends for, let me count... one, two, nine years! Thought you might have had an inkling?

ASHRAF. You're practically naked. Never mind your hair – I can see your... your legs –

SHAZIA. You don't have to look.

ASHRAF. What's happened to you, habibti?

SHAZIA. Nothing's happened! Dad! This is me. Deal with it, okay?

ASHRAF. No. You're a good Muslim girl, this is not how you were brought up –

SHAZIA. How would you know?

ASHRAF. You're better than this. This isn't you.

SHAZIA. You don't know me! You know a version of me. The version I think you can handle. I'm still never good enough though, am I? Even on my best fucking behaviour, there's always something –

ASHRAF. This swearing –

SHAZIA. Oh, pray for me, Dad. I'm gonna need it – seem to be racking up a hell of a lot of shame. Haram! Haram!

Suddenly she bursts into tears. He takes a breath. He pulls her close and hugs her.

ASHRAF. What happened?

SHAZIA *starts twisting and pulling at her engagement ring.*

SHAZIA. It's over. The wedding's off.

ASHRAF (*exploding*). Wedding?! I've never even met him!

SHAZIA. Wonder where I learned that.

Silence.

ASHRAF. You should have told me.

SHAZIA. I tried.

ASHRAF. Not very hard.

SHAZIA. I thought you'd disapprove.

ASHRAF. I do.

SHAZIA. Well, I'm hardly ecstatic about Yas... how much is she getting again? Wish I could sit about doing fuck-all!

SHAZIA *stares into space. She starts to weep again.*

ASHRAF. What has that pig-fucker son of a donkey done to you? Did he hit you?

SHAZIA. No.

ASHRAF. You know if I find out he hit you I'll castrate that cow-licking bastard.

SHAZIA. He didn't hit me.

ASHRAF. He cheat on you? Eh? My beautiful daughter not enough for that pimp whore?

SHAZIA. No. He didn't cheat on me.

ASHRAF. So what? What is so bad that this 'wedding' is off?

SHAZIA. He went home.

ASHRAF. And?

SHAZIA. And he tried to make me go with him.

ASHRAF. So you are still living separately? Alhamdulillah!

SHAZIA. No. We live together.

Silence. He lights up a cigarette.

You know that's harming yourself?

ASHRAF. I think of it more like preserving – like a smoked salmon. Anyway you can talk – you're blind like a bat drunk!

SHAZIA. Oh no no no – it's more like preserving… like a pickled egg.

Silence. They both laugh.

ASHRAF. Come. Get in, it's cold.

ASHRAF *helps her up and into the cab.*

So tell me my 'pickled egg', what is so wrong with him wanting to go home and you go home too?

SHAZIA. I was having fun! It was my choice! Just 'cause he's a boring old fart doesn't mean I have to be! And it's not the first time either – no… nope… it's a bad start – expectations, assumptions, giving me deadlines, bloody 'ultimatums', telling me what to do –

ASHRAF. So you don't do as he tells you either.

SHAZIA. No, Dad! I don't do as anyone tells me! I'm a grown woman, not a possession and I'll do what I fucking well like!

ASHRAF. Well, as long as you fucking well swear I'm sure he'll bloody fucking get the dog-shit message.

She laughs.

SHAZIA. It's the principle – it was like I didn't have a say. And… and then… what else might I not have a say in? I am not a fucking pet – I'm an independent woman! And I'll call myself whatever I bloody well want!

(*Deciding.*) Nope. It's over. This can't go on.

ASHRAF. You're right, habibti. This is a wake-up call. No good man would let you out like this.

SHAZIA. *Let* me?!

ASHRAF. Yes – he should have more pride – not want everyone to see what he has.

SHAZIA. Oh my god! This is what I'm saying –

ASHRAF. And after four years with no marriage – this is not taking you seriously.

SHAZIA. We are getting married! Well… we were.

This brings on a new wave of emotion from SHAZIA.

ASHRAF. You must stick to your own faith, your own culture –

SHAZIA. He is my culture – well half at least anyway –

ASHRAF. This is what happens. Now you have lived with him. Some sins are hard to reverse, you –

SHAZIA. But you married Mum –

ASHRAF. So you are lucky now to learn from my mistake. That 'half' culture – Bloody Cilla Black and Mr Blobby – is why you are in this situation at all. Right. So where should I take you then?

SHAZIA. I'm guessing you won't take me back to Mum's?

ASHRAF. To Preston? Now?

More crying from SHAZIA. *A deep breath from* ASHRAF.

They pull up at ASHRAF's *house.* ASHRAF *gets out to* YASMIN *waiting at the door in her dressing gown.* SHAZIA *stays in the cab.*

YASMIN. Fee eh? [*What's going on?*]

ASHRAF. It's Shazia. She's drunk, she has no clothes on and she's crying because she's had a fight with this boyfriend who she lives with.

YASMIN. He hit her?

ASHRAF. No no, nothing like that.

A beat.

I should disown her.

YASMIN. She is a grown woman – you don't own her in the first place.

A beat.

ASHRAF. She shouldn't have a boyfriend anyway. People have seen her. It's best that they split up. Then I can find her a nice Muslim husband. She's a disgrace.

YASMIN. Ashraf, beelhom maa baad arbaa sineen, wa inta maabiltohoosh lehad dilwaati. Inta el tiksif! Mish mafrood inta elli taalimha an el wafaa wa hal el mashakil...? [*Ashraf. They have been four years together and you haven't even met him. You are the disgrace. And shouldn't you teach loyalty and working through problems –*]

ASHRAF. No – I teach don't have a dog-shit western boyfriend... no, fiancé, who lets you out half-naked!

YASMIN. They're engaged?

ASHRAF. Not if I have anything to do with it.

YASMIN *peers round to see what* SHAZIA*'s doing.*

YASMIN. Don't you feel sorry for her?

ASHRAF. She has made her bed.

YASMIN. You've never made a mistake? Am I not your *second* wife?! Dakhalha el beyt. Wa khod balak minnaha. [*Let's get her in. Look after her.*]

ASHRAF. No! I am not letting that shame through my door.

YASMIN. Goodnight, Ashraf. You are the shame not coming through this door. You ring the bell when this is better. Mish ha dakhalk el beyt dah tani lehad mat titsaraf! [*You're not coming back in this house until it's done.*]

He storms back to the cab and sits in the driver's seat. He takes his beads off the mirror and looks at them a while. Long pause.

ASHRAF. Listen to me, Shazia. This Carl?

SHAZIA. Chris.

ASHRAF. Chris. What was his intention? Did he intend to prove you were his possession by behaving in that way?

SHAZIA. I guess not.

ASHRAF. What then?

SHAZIA. I guess he thought I'd had enough, probably wouldn't remember the last hour anyway, would regret staying, feel shit tomorrow and not do what I'd promised myself which was go to yoga.

A beat.

ASHRAF. I'll meet him.

SHAZIA. Really?

ASHRAF (*retracting*). No promises… just meet him is all.

A beat, retracting further.

The disrespect! He should have asked for my permission – I will be telling him this.

SHAZIA. You were in Egypt? Untraceable? Getting married?

In all of this ASHRAF's *coat has come undone and she sees his PJs. He sheepishly does up his buttons.*

Dad?

ASHRAF. Yes.

SHAZIA. Sorry Yasmin had to see me like this. She must be disgusted.

ASHRAF. She'll get over it.

Scene Ten

It's night time on Christmas Day and ASHRAF's *cab has broken down.* ASHRAF *and* YUSUF *are in the bonnet fixing it – nearly finished.*

ASHRAF. Wrench.

YUSUF *passes the wrench.* ASHRAF *tightens something.* ASHRAF *hands it back.*

Cap.

YUSUF *passes him the oil cap.* ASHRAF *screws it on and shuts the bonnet.* YUSUF *chucks* ASHRAF *the keys, who goes and sits in the driver's seat and turns on the engine. It splutters for a moment and then kicks into life. They do a little dance.*

Yes! Thank you, brother.

YUSUF. Teamwork.

ASHRAF. Happy Christmas.

YUSUF. If you like that sort of thing.

ASHRAF. Come on… he was an Arab after all!

ASHRAF *turns on the radio – some Arabic music. They dance for a minute and then as the music dims they both lean up against the bonnet exhausted and satisfied.* ASHRAF *lights up a cigarette.* YUSUF *looks longingly.* ASHRAF *offers him one.*

YUSUF. Go on then.

ASHRAF. We're celebrating – it doesn't count.

YUSUF (*lighting up*). You've always got me into trouble.

ASHRAF. What? That's not fair!

YUSUF. It's true. Remember those days in Cairo.

ASHRAF. Seems like another lifetime.

YUSUF. Remember, brother. Mama would be snoring in front of those black-and-white Omar Sharif films, and you'd be sneaking me in to watch American movies at the Cinema Metro.

ASHRAF. And every night I dreamed of seeing the Statue of Liberty. That and Coca Cola!

YUSUF. Ha! Remember when we had enough to get a few crates and so we tied all the ropes on to get them in?

ASHRAF. We pulled them up all five storeys into the window – such a spectacle – the whole street came out to watch –

YUSUF. Never seen you so proud! And Baba would be off giving horse rides to tourists at the pyramids, and the call to prayer would rumble through the house and you'd make me sneak down the stairs, out the back door –

ASHRAF. And run down the passage –

YUSUF. Past the tea shops and the trams, tourists on the donkey carts, all the way to –

ASHRAF. To Cleopatra's garden –

YUSUF. Yes! That's what we called it – just a yard really but the perfume would waft towards us through the fence, we'd breathe it in and fight to squash our faces up against the gap and –

ASHRAF. Delilah –

YUSUF. And Nanu –

ASHRAF. Would be bending over –

YUSUF. Praying.

Pause.

ASHRAF. Heaven.

YUSUF. Haram.

ASHRAF. We were kids – it doesn't count.

Pause.

YUSUF. Do you miss it?

ASHRAF. Egypt?

YUSUF. Yeah.

ASHRAF. I miss the heat. Warmth all the way through my bones.

YUSUF. Walking through crowded streets, chewing on the sugar cane.

ASHRAF. I miss the / kunafa.

YUSUF. Kunafa.

ASHRAF. Simpler times – no responsibility.

YUSUF. But everyone on the same page – the same culture –

ASHRAF. Maybe.

Pause.

YUSUF. Do you pray, brother?

ASHRAF. Yes – looking through fences –

YUSUF. No – really. Do you?

ASHRAF. Sometimes.

YUSUF. Is that enough?

ASHRAF. For who?

YUSUF. Allah I guess.

ASHRAF. I hope so. I hope he can see the bigger picture – like Cinema Metro.

YUSUF. What do you believe?

ASHRAF. That people do their best.

YUSUF. I don't know if that's enough.

Pause. YUSUF *looks down at the cigarette, stubs it out.*

Do you remember getting caught?

ASHRAF. How could I forget?

YUSUF. Five belt lashes from Baba for every cigarette you stole.

ASHRAF. Five? You got off easy!

YUSUF. I was younger –

ASHRAF. The goody two-shoes… and devout, pure – always have been.

Oum Kalthoum comes on the radio. They bask in it – singing.

YUSUF. Who you prefer? No no, how they say, yes… 'would you rather…' Delilah… with the hair… or Nanu with the… curves?

ASHRAF. You know me, brother – I'm a realist –

YUSUF. So?

ASHRAF. So… Yasmin – she's number one.

YUSUF. Bah – that is such a cop out –

ASHRAF. But Nanu is a very close second.

Scene Eleven

*It's Boxing Day in Wigan – when everyone dresses in fancy
dress.* SHAZIA *is dressed as an alien and is driving very
nervously (practice for her test),* CHRIS *is in the passenger seat
dressed as King Kong and* JEAN *is in the back in a smiley face
poo emoji costume.*

JEAN. Bloody hell that were close!

SHAZIA. Was it?

CHRIS. Nah – loads of space.

JEAN. Are you blind, lad?

CHRIS. Just 'cause you've eaten all the Christmas pies, Jean,
    doesn't mean the car's got any bigger!

JEAN. Cheeky sod. Can we at least have Magic on?

SHAZIA. No! I need to focus.

JEAN. You'll have to get used to it, I love a bit of mellow –

CHRIS. Pipe down, Jean. Eyes UP, Shaz!

JEAN. Bossy sod.

CHRIS. You're doing really well just...

    As CHRIS *says this,* SHAZIA *jerks the gear stick which
    makes a worrying sound.*

    That's third! / Stop looking down!

SHAZIA. Shit, sorry, I thought I was in one!

CHRIS. STOP LOOKING DOWN!

SHAZIA. I'M NOT!

JEAN. To be fair you were, love.

SHAZIA. Will both of yous SHUT UP.

    A moment of silence.

JEAN (*looking out the window*). At this rate I'll miss the start of the first game... it's a free drink if you get there before seven... I'll miss that too.

CHRIS. Look on the bright side – being sober might just speed up your dabbing, Jean – and if you win the bingo bonus, the snakebites'll be on you.

SHAZIA. Bit of a detox won't hurt anyway – you're still pissed from yesterday.

CHRIS. It were them shots during the Queen's speech that did it –

SHAZIA. Yeah – you went too far with that one –

JEAN. Sound like your dad... drive like him too! Ha! Brace yourself, Chris!

CHRIS. I can handle it.

JEAN. As long as you've learned the basics.

CHRIS. What do you mean?

JEAN. You know – Arabic! 'Hello.' 'Thank you.' 'Can I marry your daughter?' – that sort of thing.

CHRIS. What? Shaz, is she serious? Brake!

SHAZIA. Jesus Christ on a bike, he came out of nowhere.

JEAN. Well, it can't hurt, can it – I'll teach you... looks like we'll be here a while.

SHAZIA. Stop now. Or you can bloody get the bus with the rest of the Zimmer frame emojis if you're not careful.

JEAN. 'As-salaam alaikum' it's like their 'hello'.

CHRIS. Aslan Zalaykum, Aslan – oh – like the lion from the *Witch and the Wardrobe*?

SHAZIA *starts laughing*.

Oi – it's a thing, Shaz – read a book yeah?

JEAN. Oh look – that's Michelle, in't it?

CHRIS. Bloody hell – what's she come as? Eyes on the road, Shaz!

SHAZIA. Sorry. But I'm pissed off. She said she was gonna be my alien host, you know – so I could burst out of her belly, but it looks like she's branched out on her own. Fuck's sake.

CHRIS. You did get her a micro-dildo in the work Secret Santa – maybe she's hosting that instead –

SHAZIA. It was a joke! Can I climb out of your belly instead, Chris?

CHRIS. Where in the story does King Kong give birth to a bloody ten-stone alien?

JEAN. What are them bandages everywhere?

CHRIS. I think she's a mummy.

SHAZIA. That's racist – she's done it on purpose!

CHRIS. Brake!

JEAN *gets out of the car.*

JEAN. Wish me luck! How do I look?

CHRIS. Like crap! Ha!

JEAN. Good luck tomorrow if I don't see you later.

CHRIS. No need. You love me, don't you? Got charm for days.

JEAN. Certainly got something.

Scene Twelve

SHAZIA *goes to get in the front of the cab but* ASHRAF *locks that door from inside and winds the window down a bit. He gestures for her to get in the back. She doesn't. He winds it down a bit more to speak.*

ASHRAF. Get in the back.

SHAZIA (*getting into the back*). Yep, great start. Why do I have to get in the back?

ASHRAF. No headscarf. We agreed – Yasmin is coming.

SHAZIA. But –

ASHRAF. So now I will have Kev in the front.

SHAZIA. His name is Chris!

ASHRAF. Chris, will ride with me to the restaurant. And you will get to know Yasmin some more.

SHAZIA. Please don't be embarrassing.

ASHRAF. You don't be embarrassing.

SHAZIA. You've got loads in common… music, football –

ASHRAF. Wigan Athletic?

SHAZIA. Man U.

ASHRAF *spits in disgust.*

It's a game. Do you know where you're going?

ASHRAF. First we pick up him, and then we get Yasmin and then to the restaurant, yes?

SHAZIA. Right. It's the next right.

ASHRAF. I am aware of this, Shazia, I drive taxi for my profession.

ASHRAF *pulls over.* CHRIS *is already waiting, smiling and waving, wearing a suit.*

SHAZIA. Smile, Dad. Please.

ASHRAF *gruffly beckons* CHRIS *into the front seat next to him.*

ASHRAF. Come.

As CHRIS *gets in* ASHRAF *shuts the glass between the front and back seats.*

CHRIS. Alakazam, Ashraf, pleased to meet you.

ASHRAF. As-salaam alaikum.

(*With a cheeky grin.*) Kyle. Pleased to meet you.

SHAZIA. Dad? Dad?! What are you doing?

SHAZIA *starts banging on the window.* ASHRAF *slides it open a crack.*

ASHRAF. What is it?

SHAZIA. I just think we should all talk together.

ASHRAF. You talk too much.

CHRIS. Fair point!

ASHRAF. Do not disrespect her. Let me and Ken talk as men. And when Yasmin comes you can talk as women. About nails and Brian Gosling and suchlike.

SHAZIA. This is ridiculous.

ASHRAF *shuts the window.*

ASHRAF. You plan to marry my daughter.

CHRIS. Er, yes. Yeah, I mean, I'd love to, if that's okay with you?

ASHRAF. Will she be wearing niqab once you are wed?

CHRIS. Niqab. Er. Yeah, I'm sure she'd look great in er… niqab.

ASHRAF. Good. And when you have children will they go to mosque?

CHRIS. I mean… that's quite a way off I think – Shaz, er… Shazia wants to focus on her career a while first so –

ASHRAF. You will not be providing for her?

CHRIS. Oh, er, yes, yes of course I will, just, she's… well, she's very clever and wants to pursue her career –

ASHRAF. I see you have a good Muslim beard.

CHRIS. Yep. Yes I do…

Silence. SHAZIA *starts to bang on the window again.*

ASHRAF. Just ignore. She will tire. We can drown out.

ASHRAF *puts the radio on – some of his classic Arabic tunes. It's 'Ana Mosh Kaafir' ('I'm Not a Heathen') by Ziad Rahbani.* CHRIS *starts nodding his head along.*

You like Arab music? Rahbani?

CHRIS. Oh yeah, yeah, he's great – really catchy.

ASHRAF *pulls over –* YASMIN *is waiting at the side.*

ASHRAF. Yes, this is one of Shazia's favourites – translated means 'I am not a heathen'.

YASMIN *appears at* CHRIS*'s window in a headscarf.* CHRIS *winds it down.*

YASMIN. You are Chris! We have heard about you. As-salaam alaikum.

CHRIS *puts his hand out of the window to go for a formal handshake.*

CHRIS. Hi, Yasmin. It's a pleasure.

YASMIN. Let's go.

YASMIN *gets in the car.*

Ezayak, habibi, how are you? Good day?

SHAZIA. He's got the window shut. He wanted to talk to Chris without me, apparently.

YASMIN. Oh dear.

SHAZIA. I'm sorry I've got my hair out.

YASMIN. You look nice.

CHRIS. So... Shaz says you like the footie?

ASHRAF. Yes I do. How many Man U supporters does it take to stop a moving bus?

CHRIS. Er –

ASHRAF. Never enough. What do you call a Manchester person with no arms and legs?

CHRIS. Para–

ASHRAF. Trustworthy. What's the difference between a dead fox in the road and a dead Manchester fan?

CHRIS. I think this is a bit –

ASHRAF (*cracking up at himself*). Skid marks in front of the fox! Ha!

A beat.

Go on then. Your turn. You must have a joke? You like to laugh?

CHRIS. Nah, you're alright.

ASHRAF. Come on, man! Even Shazia has good jokes! Anything?

CHRIS. Alright, alright – if we're okay with doing *personal* jokes how about this... how does a Muslim close the door?

ASHRAF. My religion is not –

CHRIS. Islam's it! Get it?! Islam? He slams?!

YASMIN *taps on the window.* ASHRAF *opens it a bit.*

YASMIN. Let's all talk together, no? I want to meet Chris.

ASHRAF. Oh, okay yes. Chris, why don't you tell my wife the joke you just made about Islam?

CHRIS. Nah, mate, you're alright. You've given away the punch line now anyway.

YASMIN. Chris, Shazia says you are teacher? Children with special needs?

CHRIS. That's right.

YASMIN. Very difficult.

CHRIS. Nay, it's brilliant. Got a well funny bunch at the moment. There's one lad's got a feeding tube up his nose, and I've got another one with a sort of fetish for tubes – keeps trying to pull it out – constantly chasing him round classroom. Luckily the one with the tube is a bit faster 'cause he's got a dead posh supersonic wheelchair thing – like Lewis Hamilton he is… broom broom!!

YASMIN. Humour very important! Yes! This is how I deal with Ashraf! As they say 'laughter is better than the drugs'.

ASHRAF (*quickly changing the subject*). How were your studies today? Still struggling?

CHRIS. Studies?

YASMIN. Yes – I had been studying my driving theory. But I have some good news.

CHRIS. Go on?

YASMIN. I passed! Today. At the test centre!

ASHRAF. You didn't tell me you booked the test.

YASMIN. I didn't want to disappoint if I fail.

SHAZIA. Yasmin, that's amazing!

ASHRAF. Yes – Yasmin has been here three months and passed. What is your excuse?

CHRIS. I'm teaching her.

SHAZIA. Yeah, I even reversed out the car park the other day, didn't I?

ASHRAF. Car park and Mesnes Park very different…

SHAZIA (*correcting the pronounciation*). Mesnes Park, Dad.

ASHRAF. And don't get me started on Saddle Junction –

YASMIN. You will get there, Shazia.

SHAZIA. You know your English is so much better, Yas–

YASMIN. I have the citizenship test next.

CHRIS. You'll be fine – your English is great!

YASMIN. Thank you but the English is not it. I need to know about Henry Eighth daughter – the Bloody Mary –

ASHRAF. Yasmin!

CHRIS. That's her name –

ASHRAF. You must not defend this language –

YASMIN. And for how many years you defend against Romans, and what bird you eat on your Christmas festival –

ASHRAF. Turkey of course – this is easy.

YASMIN. Oh yes – how you say? A slice of the cake?

CHRIS. Thinking about it though, some people like a ham on Christmas Day –

SHAZIA. Chris!

CHRIS. What?

SHAZIA. We don't eat ham!

CHRIS. You don't celebrate Christmas either!

ASHRAF. Someone has to drive the drunk idiots on Christmas Day!

CHRIS. Seriously though – no bacon? You don't know what you're missing!

SHAZIA. Chris!

CHRIS. What?!

YASMIN. Swine is unclean, haram.

CHRIS. Yeah, probably if you hang it up in the desert heat for five days, but if you get it from the cold counter at Lidl it –

SHAZIA. For fuck's sake, Chris!

CHRIS. What?! It's not like I'm asking him if he were bezzy mates with Bin Laden before he died!

ASHRAF *pulls over.*

YASMIN. Ashraf.

ASHRAF. Out. Get out of my car now.

CHRIS (*getting out of the car*). What? I were saying I *wasn't* asking you that, I was just trying to explain how great a bacon –

ASHRAF. OUT!

Interval.

Scene Thirteen

CHRIS *is driving and* SHAZIA *is in the passenger seat.*
They've just been for their regular date night – 'Groupon
Tuesdays' which was his choice this week – watching Lawrence
of Arabia *– in an attempt to make it up to her. An awkward*
silence.

SHAZIA. I'm not sure that counts as a 'Groupon Tuesday'
anyway –

CHRIS. Shaz – they aren't going to be playing classic films
with Arabic settings in the bloody Empire are they... Uncle
Gary's sixty-inch is the best we were gonna get.

SHAZIA. Whatever.

A frosty beat, CHRIS *desperate to make up.*

CHRIS. So... do you feel closer to your roots?

SHAZIA. Give over.

CHRIS. I certainly do – I love it – it's mystical, exotic.

A beat.

Listen, can you please just drop it now? I'm trying, I've
learned my lesson and I will be making amends with your
dad, I promise.

SHAZIA. It's too late, Chris. It's fucked.

CHRIS. No. No, it's not. I can fix it, I'll bring him round. And,
and I can get into this stuff... I can. Trust me.

SHAZIA. Stuff. Right.

A beat.

CHRIS (*being cultured*). I think more films should have intervals.
It would enable creators to have more epic visions,
unencumbered with the ninety-minute format, don't you think?

SHAZIA (*thawing slightly*). I guess I was glad of having a slash
mid-story – without being bollocked by you for it.

CHRIS. One for the marriage manifesto – pop it down!

A beat. SHAZIA *doesn't want to think about the marriage.*

Seriously though, with the film – did you get a sense of home... you know – did your genes sort of quiver seeing Cairo for the first time?

SHAZIA. Nope.

CHRIS. You know what, I didn't know he was gay either? Lawrence. Or do you reckon that was just for the film?

SHAZIA. What?

CHRIS. Homosexual.

SHAZIA. Chris, I know what gay is... who are you talking about?

CHRIS. Lawrence... of Arabia! Your homeland... Arabia?

SHAZIA. I did not get that.

CHRIS. Polish your gaydar, Shaz – it couldn't of been more in your face.

SHAZIA. Bloody hell.

CHRIS. Spoke good Arabic too – Lawrence... didn't he... you never thought to learn?

SHAZIA. I was learning. Till my mum and dad... well. I've got a few words anyway.

CHRIS. Great. We can learn together.

Silence. CHRIS *looks at* SHAZIA *– they might go into a deep and meaningful here but instead:*

SHAZIA. No bloody women in it AT ALL.

CHRIS. That's the patriarchy right there.

SHAZIA. Er... yeah.

Pause.

CHRIS. It's weird – you know there wasn't that much plot was there – I mean, I can't really talk about what happened… more – it was like a feeling like… I think we should go there…

SHAZIA. Right.

CHRIS. Haven't booked the honeymoon yet you know…

SHAZIA. Right.

CHRIS. Next on the list – *The Mummy*. Trust me, Shaz, I'll sort it.

SHAZIA. Right.

Scene Fourteen

A notification beeps on ASHRAF's *phone, he sees it and hurriedly turns on the radio.*

RADIO. And now to sport: Wigan Athletic have beaten Millwall at home by two goals to one in the Sky Bet championship this afternoon in a tight-fought game.

ASHRAF. Yes!

RADIO. Though the success of the match was marred by racist chanting from the away supporters following the second goal by midfielder Gavin Massey.

ASHRAF *turns off the radio, agitated.*

ASHRAF. Bloody hooligans.

He picks up the phone to call YASMIN.

Salaam. I missed the party? I'm sorry I forgot – match day… Millwall – very busy, yes. Listen, don't go into town today. (*Pause.*) Okay. Okay. Yasmin, but maybe don't wear your scarf – I don't mind. Okay salaam salaam. (*Pause.*) And get me some biscuits… bourbons, or dark chocolate Hobnobs. Yes. Just one more pick-up then I'll be home.

ASHRAF *lights a fag and turns on the engine.*

Scene Fifteen

A string of calls going into voicemails – people can't get hold of ASHRAF.

VOICEMAIL 1 (YUSUF). Brother – where are you? Call me back!

VOICEMAIL 2 (YASMIN). Ashraf, where are you? One pick-up you said?

VOICEMAIL 3 (YUSUF.) I hear Shazia has a boyfriend who she wants to marry and you two have met? What is happening? Call me?

VOICEMAIL 4 (JEAN). Now listen, I was chatting to Joan the other day and her nephew, Charlie, who works for this fast-food place. I were telling 'im about your sauce and he were dead interested. So next time you pick me up, bring a few bottles for me and I'll pass it on. And I won't ask for commission 'cause Shaz worries about you anyway, but don't say I never do anything for you, eh? And how's the new wife? Enjoying picking up your hundreds of half-drunk coffee mugs? Anyway, just gimme a bell.

VOICEMAIL 5 (YUSUF). Brother – you can't be ignoring me forever – we work together! Don't worry okay – we will deal with this as a community – you are not alone. Oh, and Hafifah says you're one car payment behind – let's talk okay?

VOICEMAIL 6 (YASMIN). Ashraf? Ashraf?

Scene Sixteen

ASHRAF *has been beaten up and his cab is in tatters. He falls
out of the cab onto the pavement outside his house, breathing
heavily. He takes a moment to try and smarten himself up.*
YASMIN *comes out.*

YASMIN. Ya lahwi! Hasal eeh? [*My darling! What happened?*]

ASHRAF. I'm sorry.

YASMIN. Hasal eeh? [*What happened?*]

ASHRAF. It's fine. I will be fine, it –

YASMIN. Ashan Khatri. [*Please.*]

  A beat.

ASHRAF. They. They got in the cab. Wanted to go to
   Anderton's in town. Angry with the result. Asked who I
   supported – I lied. They said I wasn't their mate. I said I am
   good person and to please calm down. They said I was
   friends with ISIS, that I should go back to Syria and that they
   would burn me and stuff my face with bacon. I ask them to
   leave the taxi. I try to film it, to stop them – make them
   leave. They drag me out of the taxi and start to smash, cut
   the seats. I try to pull one off and he slams my eye with his
   elbow. I am hurt and they are big, strong men. There is
   nothing I can do. I have to stand there while they destroy
   my... my business, my life.

  Silence.

  I am so sorry, Yasmin.

YASMIN. Habibi, wala yehimak, rabina shahid, elhamdo lellah.
   [*My love, don't worry, God is our witness, thanks be to God.*]

ASHRAF. I should not have brought you here for this. I have
   nothing to offer –

YASMIN. That is not true! You have shared everything with
   me –

ASHRAF. It's not enough. You deserve better. I am old...
   weak –

YASMIN. No, you deserve better. That taxi is not your life and neither are those stupid men. I am and Shazia is. These pigs can rot in their own shit. We will mend taxi, your eye will mend, and when you are on top of your feet we will launch your business. Together.

Pause.

Come, Ashraf – you are practically British – what do they say? Keep the calm and carry it on. We must carry. Stiff lips. Life is short – this is the lesson – we grasp it now yes, six months we will be Richard Branson. Yes?

Pause.

Yes?

ASHRAF. As long as you know that I am the boss.

YASMIN. Yes. Now let's get you inside, boss man. I have Hobnobs.

ASHRAF. Thank you.

YASMIN. You are hero.

Scene Seventeen

We see YASMIN *approach the car with a hand-held Hoover and cleaning products. She is tidying up after the attack. There's glass everywhere and the car is a state. She takes a moment to look around the car.*

There are mugs everywhere. She starts trying to stack them. She finds an old plastic bag and makes a bin.

The same happens with old copies of the Daily Star. *She reads a headline out loud.*

She turns the page – sees the page 7 girl staring back at her.

She stuffs the papers into a bin bag then reaches under his chair to find empty boxes of cigarettes stuffed under the seat.

She gets out gaffa tape and begins to mend the ripped seats. She has made covers to make the car look nice.

She wipes down the taxi radio and accidentally switches it on and can hear YUSUF *talking to other people. She sits in the driver's seat and pretends to pick up a passenger.*

YASMIN. Where you off to, mate? No problems... you having a nice day? The weather is nice...

She gets out ASHRAF's *prayer beads from her pocket and puts them back up proudly on the mirror.*

Scene Eighteen

We see YASMIN *in the driver's seat of the taxi. She is tying her headscarf into more of a modern style, like a bun. She applies her lipstick.*

SHAZIA *gets into the car.*

SHAZIA. As-salaam alaikum. I didn't expect you to be driving.

YASMIN. Yes, now I passed, here I am on the insurance.

SHAZIA. Great.

YASMIN. When your dad is better he will teach you.

SHAZIA. Erm... no. Better?

YASMIN. Yes... this is why I call you.

SHAZIA. What's wrong with him?

YASMIN. He had some bad people in his taxi.

SHAZIA. What?

YASMIN. Don't worry. He is 'in the mend'.

SHAZIA. What did they do? I'll kill them. Why didn't he tell me? When did this happen? Why didn't you call me?

YASMIN. Please, we didn't want you to worry. He is okay.

SHAZIA. I thought he wasn't talking to me cos of Chris... I... What did they do?

YASMIN. They smash the windows and with a key cut the seats.

SHAZIA. Was it racist? What is a racist attack? Is he hurt?

YASMIN. He is lucky, believe me, but his eye is bad and he can't drive.

SHAZIA *wells up*.

SHAZIA. Fucking dipshit dumbass uneducated fuck-stains. Did you go to the police?

YASMIN. Yes, but they have not found them yet. Don't worry. God will have his plans for them, Inshallah.

Silence.

SHAZIA. What will you do for money? Do you need help? Look, I can go to the cash machine –

YASMIN. No.

SHAZIA. But how will you –

YASMIN. We have some donations through – from the mosque – see – religion is like family, it –

SHAZIA. But that won't last long will it, how will you –

The radio crackles.

Wait... you're not driving this thing, are you?

Silence.

Yasmin?

YASMIN. It's fine. I have driver's licence and satnav. It's good... I'm getting to know Wigan.

SHAZIA. What? You don't have a taxi licence. You can't just pick up people. And are you actually insured on this car?

YASMIN. It's okay. As long as we have a good heart, God will protect us.

SHAZIA. Okay... I'm not sure if the police will see it that way. I don't think I can let you do this.

YASMIN. Too late.

SHAZIA. How late?

YASMIN. Two days. I make very good money.

SHAZIA. But –

YASMIN. I need to replace windscreen and windows... I have to find money to pay back... the sewing it's not enough. So when your father is better he can come straight back to taxi.

SHAZIA. I can't believe he let you do this!

A look.

He doesn't know?!

YASMIN. And I save – for his spicy sauce. I spoke to Wigan market for a pitch.

Pause.

He is too good for this taxi.

Pause.

I believe the saying is 'what he doesn't know didn't kill him'. I can trust you. Yes?

SHAZIA. Yes. And while we're telling secrets... I never wear a headscarf. And I don't pray. I don't even know the proper prayer thing.

YASMIN. What? This is bad. We must take you to the mosque to pray for forgiveness. Straight away.

A beat.

Shazia, I don't care. You are my family. I know all this anyway... your father is bad liar!

The radio crackles. We hear YUSUF *talking to a different driver about a job.*

You know what that Yusuf wants yes? He nags your father for you to marry that Omar's son!

SHAZIA. What the one with the eye?

YASMIN (*with a wink*). And kind heart.

SHAZIA. Yeah... yeah well... I'm sure he's lovely –

YASMIN. As is Chris... ignorant yes, like the bull in the Chinese shop maybe, but he has good heart – working with those kids and –

SHAZIA. Do you think he'll come round?

YASMIN. Ashraf? It's not important. You love each other, yes?

SHAZIA. We do.

YASMIN. Then that is it.

A beat.

SHAZIA. Thanks, Yas... for understanding – I thought you were a lot more, you know strict.

YASMIN. People will find Allah in their own way, if they are meant to.

SHAZIA. Yas... I think I want to do the henna and stuff, for my wedding – a nod to Egypt and Dad and that. Will you help me?

YASMIN. I would be honoured.

A beat.

Yallah, before we go home we pick up Mr Patel – let's get him before whoever Yusuf sends. As the saying goes 'one bird in hand is worth two big bushes'.

Both of their phones go at the same time. It's a video from ASHRAF *of a goat with a monkey riding on its back.*

More bastard goats!

Scene Nineteen

It's the day of SHAZIA*'s dress fitting.* SHAZIA *and* JEAN *are in the car waiting for* YASMIN *to get in.*

SHAZIA. Just be friendly.

JEAN. Course! I've got nowt against her – poor woman.

SHAZIA. And don't slag off Dad.

JEAN. Like I would. I'm surprised he's let her come after what happened with Chris... bloody dickhead.

SHAZIA. I don't know that he knows – he's still laid up, maybe she didn't bother him with it. Shhhh, here she is.

YASMIN *gets in the back seat of the car.*

YASMIN. Hello, habibti. Hello, Jean – I have heard so much about you.

JEAN. Yeah – I bet you bloody have.

SHAZIA. Mum!

Silence.

YASMIN. I knew you will pass your test – I prayed – you're very good, clever girl.

JEAN. You're too close to the kerb on this side.

Silence.

YASMIN. Jean – Ashraf said that you may be walking Shazia to the aisle? I like this – very modern, yes?

JEAN. What?

SHAZIA. Nothing. No, Yas – I'm walking myself – far as I'm concerned I don't belong to anyone but me so I'm giving myself away.

YASMIN. Oh yes! Very good.

A beat.

You must be excited to try on the dress?

SHAZIA. Yeah! Well, I hope I haven't put too much weight on – the diet's not really gone to plan.

JEAN. Shut it, you, I've seen more fat on a greasy chip.

YASMIN. Yes, you're very small… like stick insect, yes?

Silence.

SHAZIA. So… Yasmin, what have you been up to today?

YASMIN. Just some cleaning.

JEAN. Picking up his cups of half-drunk tea and bloody red-tops I bet – lazy sod.

SHAZIA. Mum! What did I say?

JEAN. Next left.

SHAZIA. I know.

Pause.

YASMIN. Shazia, I have some jewellery for you for the wedding, your Aunt Nadia sends it. Nice Egyptian gold –

JEAN. No need – she's already got –

SHAZIA (*eyeballing* JEAN). Great, I'll take a look.

Pause.

JEAN. Eee – Nadia, how is she? Still got her pigeons?

SHAZIA. Pigeons? Gross –

YASMIN. No – they're nice –

JEAN. S'true – some of them birds were bloody stunning!

YASMIN. Her 'children'.

JEAN. When I was there she had about a hundred.

YASMIN. This is nothing! When I left she has four hundred, last month she wins big prize, she has one big one called Mubarak and he can do a flip like gymnast.

A beat.

She never married though – it's sad.

JEAN. No way – too wise… pigeons don't fuck up your life.

SHAZIA. Mum!

Pause.

She sounds ace – Nadia.

JEAN. That's who you get your middle name from.

SHAZIA. I didn't know that!

JEAN. Yeah – always liked her – made a crackin' brew – what was it she always said? Shaay –

JEAN *and* YASMIN. Shaay tozbot dimaghi!

JEAN. It were proper black, with funny little bead things in it. 'Shaay tozbot dimaghi' – means 'tea to solve your problems' – being married to Ashraf it was well bloody needed – eh, Yas?!

SHAZIA. Mum!

YASMIN. There are certain… how you say… challenges, yes.

JEAN. Challenges! You're a better woman than me!

Pause.

SHAZIA. Anyway… I didn't know you spoke Arabic.

JEAN. You didn't ask!

(*To* YASMIN.) 'Saat et zahma…'

YASMIN.… 'Ye tahro el uleyt laama.'Did Nadia teach you this? This very naughty!

They both laugh – it means 'in times of chaos is when they try to circumsise the blind fool' – a well used phrase.

SHAZIA. What does it mean?

JEAN. How are you finding Wigan?

YASMIN. Yes good, the people here are friendly.

JEAN. Bloody hell – look at Ashraf. God… if I get wind of who
did it I'll kneecap 'em myself… then tie them up in my
basement and then castrate the fuckers… slowly… with a
blunt bloody butter knife!

Pause.

YASMIN. Jean, you must come to the house after the fitting.
I will make you some nice tea.

JEAN. Sounds great.

SHAZIA. I'd like that too, sounds nice.

SHAZIA *pulls over.*

We're here.

JEAN. Alive too! Alhamdulillah!

YASMIN *laughs.*

SHAZIA. Shut it.

They start to get out of the car.

Please, God, let it fit.

JEAN. If I'm honest, I were quite surprised you went for white
– you're not exactly a –

SHAZIA. Mum!

YASMIN. I had white dress too, Shazia!

JEAN. Fair play… I did and all! Ha!

Scene Twenty

ASHRAF *is sat in the same spot. Still can't drive, still not healed. There's a collection of stuff around him – mugs, wrappers, fag butts, etc. and lots of letters that look like bills.*

ASHRAF *takes his beads off the mirror. He hesitates before he picks up his phone and dials another number.*

YUSUF. As-salaam alaikum, Ashraf.

ASHRAF. Alaikum salaam. How are you?

YUSUF. I should be asking you this. How is your eye? Have you been resting?

ASHRAF. Yes. Thank you.

YUSUF. Omar has said you can have one of his son's eye patches if you want!

Pause.

Really though, brother – you okay?

ASHRAF. I need a favour – the car payments I owe you, I can't work for a while – not till my eye –

YUSUF. You have no rainy-day savings? No back-up?

ASHRAF. I just got married, Yusuf, I've been working day and night you know this –

YUSUF. Let me speak to Hafifah –

ASHRAF. Thank you!

YUSUF. I'll tell her to delay for a week okay?

ASHRAF. Just a week?

YUSUF. Another week – you are already behind. So two weeks, with no late fee.

ASHRAF. Yes, okay, that's very kind.

YUSUF. Okay… get better, yes?

ASHRAF. I'll do my best.

Awkward silence.

YUSUF. This should never have happened – if there is
something we can do, you must say.

ASHRAF. You've been very generous. Okay. Thank you for
your time.

JEAN *strides over to the car.*

JEAN (*acknowledging how he looks*). Bloody hell. Pigs.

(*Then quickly.*) What's this about you not walking her down
the aisle?

ASHRAF. Hello, ex-wife. Yes, I am fine thank you so much –
very healthy. And you?

JEAN. I bloody mean it! What's wrong with you? She's your
daughter – she loves you to bits – think how much it'd
mean –

ASHRAF. No. If people find out, the community –

JEAN. Oh for God's sake – you married me – I'm about as
Muslim as Bernard bloody Manning! Do what *you* want – it
doesn't matter what those extremists –

ASHRAF. They're not bloody extremists, they're devout –

JEAN. They can be all of the forty virgins rolled into one for all
I care – life's short – you're lucky to still be here – just walk
your daughter down the bloody aisle –

ASHRAF. You are not the boss of me any more!

JEAN. There were three of us in that marriage. Don't let Yusuf
ruin this too.

She stomps off.

ASHRAF. Bloody rude fishwife nag-horse.

ASHRAF *leans on the car. Deep in contemplation.*

Scene Twenty-One

YASMIN *is in the taxi. We hear* YUSUF *say something about The Galleries,* YASMIN *fires up the engine. Her phone rings, she picks up.*

YASMIN. Yusuf.

YUSUF. Yasmin, good, I was hoping to speak to you after mosque but you left so quickly.

YASMIN. Yes – I needed to get back to Ashraf – he's still very sore.

YUSUF. Right.

YASMIN. Right.

YUSUF. When do you think he'll be driving again?

YASMIN. Tomorrow. He is determined. It is too soon, but he is stubborn.

Pause.

YUSUF. You need to talk to him, Yasmin.

YASMIN. I do – every day!

YUSUF. About this wedding. You know it's haram.

YASMIN. Shazia is not a practising Muslim.

YUSUF. At the moment.

YASMIN. Yes.

Pause.

YUSUF. Yasmin, you and I both know how this goes – we will lose her for good if this happens.

YASMIN. Who is this 'we'.

YUSUF. Can't you see? If this goes ahead we'll have to disown her –

YASMIN. Another 'we'.

YUSUF. You more than anyone should understand – the community will not accept this –

YASMIN. Which community? Didn't you know your mama has offered a place for Shazia's honeymoon?

YUSUF. Sending blessings from Egypt and having to face people at the mosque very different.

A beat.

Mama's not here.

YASMIN. No.

Pause.

YUSUF. Look what happened to Ashraf – we need to stick together –

YASMIN. What happened to Ashraf? I'll tell you what happened – *you* – always hold him back – getting in his head –

YUSUF. For his own good – he's a dreamer, Yasmin!

YASMIN. Dreams and ambition, it's different.

YUSUF. There are things you don't know, Yasmin. I have had to support Ashraf financially. That taxi –

YASMIN. I do know, Yusuf. I know he's paying instalments to you. I know he's been struggling to make payments. I know you charge interest. I know you don't support his ambitions to have his own business.

YUSUF. The sauce? I thought you would be a good influence. I campaigned for Mama to match you.

YASMIN. Well, thank you for your help.

Pause.

YUSUF. Yasmin, I am sorry, but please think of Shazia. Think of our brothers here in Wigan – since you have arrived it's like Ashraf is complete again, and now?

YASMIN. Now what?

YUSUF. Ya Allah, Yasmin!

YASMIN. Sorry, Yusuf, I have to go –

YUSUF. Where?

YASMIN. The Galleries.

YUSUF. That's strange – I've just sent a car –

> YASMIN *starts the engine.*

It's not... it's you? Been cutting in on my jobs. You?

YASMIN. I don't know what you're talking about.

YUSUF. Does Ashraf know about this?

YASMIN. Oh go playing with yourself, Yusuf, yes?

> *She hangs up.*

Scene Twenty-Two

ASHRAF *is sitting on the street next to the cab, smoking. He has an eye patch on and looks terrible.* CHRIS *approaches.*

ASHRAF. I am busy.

CHRIS (*referencing* ASHRAF's *face after the attack*). Bloody hell. Fucking pigs.

ASHRAF. I said I'm busy.

CHRIS. Peace offering. Breakfast.

> *He hands over what looks like a bacon sandwich.*

ASHRAF. Is this some sort of sick joke?

CHRIS. What? No no! Got it from Oliver Twist's. It's facon.

ASHRAF. Facon.

CHRIS. Facon. Fake bacon?

ASHRAF. Yes?

CHRIS. Yep! All the goodness of bacon, none of the shame.

ASHRAF. Are you sure?

CHRIS. Er yeah.

ASHRAF. Then why not sell this in the halal shops?

CHRIS. Well, it's not meat, is it? It's more for the beardy vegans, I think.

ASHRAF. Nothing wrong with beards.

CHRIS. I know. Try it, then!

ASHRAF. Okay.

He bites into it.

CHRIS. Is it rank? Sorry. Should've known it'd be –

ASHRAF. No – no! Wait, it just needs something a little extra, hang on!

He goes to his car and gets out a pot of his sauce and pours it on.

Delicious. It just needed Ashraf's special sauce! I should sell this at the mosque – would make a killing! Facon Butties. Spicy Facon. Finger Lickin' Facon. Take On Some Facon.

CHRIS. Facon Fac-off?

ASHRAF. What?

CHRIS. Never mind.

ASHRAF. Right.

CHRIS. Ashraf. Listen, I really am sorry about before. I was nervous and, well, I put my foot in it – it was racist and wrong and… and I'm learning – and… I'm nothing like those dickheads who did this… and I'm just, I'm sorry okay?

ASHRAF. Okay.

CHRIS. Phew, good. Okay. There was something I wanted to ask, something I should have asked a long time ago.

ASHRAF. Yes?

CHRIS. Would it be okay if I married Shaz? With you I mean. Do I have your permission?

ASHRAF. Does she know you're here?

CHRIS. Er... no.

ASHRAF. She would say the permission is not for me to give.

CHRIS. Yeah. Yeah she would.

ASHRAF. But since she's not here, then I will consider it.

CHRIS. What?

ASHRAF. Mixed-culture marriages very difficult. I know this.

CHRIS. I love her though, and I know you do too, and it's what she wants, and –

ASHRAF. Oh bloody hell, fine, whatever, just stop talking yes? You have the permission.

CHRIS. Thanks! And as I said, I really am sorry about the whole Christmas ham thing. I didn't know it was such a big deal.

ASHRAF. The Manchester United is more of a concern.

CHRIS. Here's one. What does a Wigan Athletic fan do when his team wins the league?

ASHRAF. Take his rightful place in history –

CHRIS. Turn off the PlayStation!

ASHRAF. Bloody dickhead.

Scene Twenty-Three

The car is full of energy drinks and empty coffee cups.
ASHRAF's *still wearing an eye patch. He's undone quite a few*
buttons revealing the vest underneath his shirt. The song 'Bad
Boys' by Inner Circle is on and he's singing manically.

SHAZIA *gets in the car, she looks a bit alarmed.* CHRIS *tries*
to show his improvement.

CHRIS. As-salaam alaikum, Ashraf.

ASHRAF. You too, brother. You like reggae, man? This bit's for
    you, Shaz!

He sings again until:

SHAZIA. Dad! Stop!

ASHRAF. It's true though, habibti – you wanna let go, and I got
    to let you, innit!

CHRIS. Ashraf, are you okay?

ASHRAF. Oh yeah, just working a lot, man – missed a lot of
    work innit – bills to pay, so got to be a pirate for a while
    yeah? Sailing these treacherous Wigan road-seas to bring
    home the booty... bounty, yes?

SHAZIA. Should you really be working?

ASHRAF (*snapping*). When will you learn you do not question
    your father. Of course I should be bloody dog-shit working.

A slightly awkward silence, ASHRAF *nods along to the beat.*

CHRIS. So what's with the reggae then, mate?

ASHRAF. A gift from one of the drug dealers I pick up – I told
    him about how I used to smoke so much weed I got paranoid
    and he left it as a parting gift.

CHRIS. You used to smoke weed?!

ASHRAF. Course bloody not! But you got to fit in, man.
    Always fit in.

CHRIS. So you don't mind picking up dealers?

ASHRAF. Business is business and if you need to provide for my Shazia you better learn that quick-smart like Usain Bolt.

A beat.

Anyway, it is for Allah to judge, not me. They don't bother me, I don't bother them. Simples.

A pause.

You don't like reggae?

CHRIS. I do, yeah, I love reggae.

ASHRAF. Well, sing then, boy! Come on, habibti, you know this one!

He starts to sing 'One Love/People Get Ready' by Bob Marley & The Wailers.

CHRIS *and* SHAZIA *join in – reluctantly at first.*

ASHRAF *pulls over and suddenly looks incredibly tired and drawn. He scrabbles around for some paracetamol but there are none left. He pulls himself together.*

Come, let's go, Yasmin has been cooking for you all day.

SHAZIA. Just a sec, Dad.

ASHRAF. What, what is this? Yasmin will put my head in her blender if we are late. You know she's passed her citizenship test?

SHAZIA. What?! No! Oh my God, Dad. That's great news!

ASHRAF. Yes. I am stuck with her for good. How you say… hag-ridden?! Come!

SHAZIA. Dad. She won't mind a couple of minutes. There's something I want to ask you.

ASHRAF (*snapping*). For the love of all that is holy, Shazia, I've told you I cannot walk you down the aisle of this heathen wedding! What will people say?

SHAZIA. I know. I wasn't going to ask that. I was just thinking –

ASHRAF. What? What were you thinking!

SHAZIA. About all the fun times we've had in this taxi… singing, shouting at people, laughing –

ASHRAF. You're right. It has not all been work and drug dealers and racist fucking English and such. This old donkey has served us well.

SHAZIA. Exactly. And I totally get that you can't walk me down the aisle… but… well, I wanted to ask if you might just drive me to my wedding… in this. This donkey would do me proud.

A beat to think. This is the perfect compromise.

ASHRAF. Okay… okay yes! I will shine her up, good as new, put the ribbons on there –

SHAZIA. Thanks, Dad!

ASHRAF. Now come. You must act surprised when Yasmin breaks this news, she will gut me like a fish if I told you first.

Scene Twenty-Four

ASHRAF (*now without the eye patch*) *is out of the car, smoking, enjoying the sunshine on his break, leaning against the bonnet.* YUSUF *comes over and joins him in a mirror of their previous scene.* ASHRAF *offers* YUSUF *a cigarette.*

YUSUF. No. Thank you.

ASHRAF. Beautiful day.

YUSUF. Yes.

A pause. They both know what's coming and almost elongate this moment of quiet on purpose.

I hear it's going ahead.

ASHRAF. Yes.

YUSUF. This is very grave, brother. I am sorry.

ASHRAF. Yes. Me too.

YUSUF. The Koran is very clear on this: 'Believers should not take Kafirs as friends in preference to other believers. Those who do this will have none of Allah's protection and will only have themselves as guards.'

ASHRAF. I have read it. Thanks.

YUSUF. So?

ASHRAF. So… Shazia is a good Muslim girl, and Chris is a kind man and they love each other –

YUSUF. You know that this is forbidden.

ASHRAF. What would you have me do?

YUSUF. You know that too.

ASHRAF. I think it's time you looked to the Koran for yourself. What about leaving aside what does not concern you?

YUSUF. You are my brother, Ashraf, of course it concerns me.

A beat.

I hear you're planning to attend.

ASHRAF. I'm just driving her.

YUSUF. In the taxi? If you go through with this we will have to call in the loan. No more taxi –

ASHRAF. Yusuf, listen carefully because in the words of that brilliant Muslim programme, *Allo Allo*, I will say this only once. Shazia is twice the man you will ever be and so is Chris and I'm fairly sure that Allah can work that out.

YUSUF. You know Yasmin's been driving your taxi? Your women are not in your control.

ASHRAF. Of course I know. Bloody just fuck off!

ASHRAF storms into the taxi and puts the keys in to drive off. YUSUF rushes round to get in the other side. ASHRAF tries to reach over and push down the knob to lock it but YUSUF gets in in time.

Get out of my taxi.

YUSUF. It's not your taxi.

YUSUF reaches over to try and pull the keys out of the ignition. A struggle, which turns into a physical fight. Eventually ASHRAF manages to fall out of the driver's door on to the pavement, for the second time in recent weeks. He's breathless and broken. YUSUF starts the engine. ASHRAF is on his knees.

ASHRAF. Please, please, brother.

YUSUF. Talk to her – please – there's still time.

ASHRAF. Please.

YUSUF pulls the keys out of the ignition and gets out of the car.

Please.

YUSUF. You choose this.

A beat.

You choose to walk *away* from your religion… your community.

ASHRAF takes a deep breath.

ASHRAF. No. I walk *towards* my daughter… my family.

A beat.

Please, brother. Just one last journey.

YUSUF places the keys firmly in ASHRAF's hands. Or drops keys.

YUSUF. Goodbye.

Scene Twenty-Five

SHAZIA *and* CHRIS *are waiting in the taxi. There's a bit of an atmosphere. The car radio is playing Arabic music.* SHAZIA *has henna up both her arms.*

CHRIS. He's taking his time.

SHAZIA. Probably a number two.

CHRIS. Nice.

Silence.

Look I've said I'm sorry. I've taken it off Facebook – no one's going to see it.

SHAZIA. I know.

CHRIS. They were stupid. They just thought it would be funny.

SHAZIA. I know they did. They're fucking ignorant. I just can't understand why you didn't stop them.

CHRIS. It's my stag do. I can't just say 'Sorry, guys, I can't wear a burka today because it might offend Shaz's stepmother,' can I?

SHAZIA. It's offended me! And it's not even a burka it's a fucking hijab.

CHRIS. You always used to laugh at this sort of thing –

SHAZIA. Yeah? Well, I'm growing up –

CHRIS. And what's all this stuff on your arm anyway?

SHAZIA. It's henna.

CHRIS. Right. Course.

SHAZIA. What?

CHRIS. Nothing!

SHAZIA. Seriously, Chris. What is it?

CHRIS. It's just.

Pause.

Well, what are you gonna wear? On the actual wedding?

SHAZIA. It's a secret, isn't it.

CHRIS. Yeah. Sure, but, just – I know you've been getting closer to your culture and that's great, but I just – well –

SHAZIA. Well what, Chris?

CHRIS. I'd just rather know, you know, if you're planning on rocking up in a burka... hijab or whatever –

SHAZIA. Right.

CHRIS. Fuck's sake.

Silence.

I'm never going to say the right thing, Shaz. I'm a blunt instrument and you know that. I just. It's all new. And I know it's a big part of you and it's important and Lord knows I love the falafel and stuff, it's just... when we met I didn't see any of that. I just saw you. And I've been brought up very... well... white. And my mates and family are even worse than me, and I guess I'm scared it's all going to be a bit well, alien, different and not what anyone expects – I mean – what if they put their foot in it? All I really want to do is just marry my best friend. So...

SHAZIA. I love you, Chris. I'm wearing a white dress.

CHRIS. Cool.

SHAZIA. With a white lace niqab.

CHRIS. Right. Great, that's great.

SHAZIA. Joke! I'm joking!

CHRIS. Okay. Phew. Fuck's sake.

Scene Twenty-Six

It's the morning of the wedding and ASHRAF *is having a fag.*
YASMIN *comes out with ribbons and a rag to polish the taxi.*
ASHRAF *stubs out the fag quickly and wafts the smoke.*

YASMIN. Ashraf.

ASHRAF. Sorry. Just… this wedding. Stress.

YASMIN. I know.

    ASHRAF *surveys the taxi.*

ASHRAF. She's been a faithful friend.

YASMIN. One last journey.

ASHRAF. He might let me keep her.

YASMIN. Don't hold your breathing eh – you will suffocate!

    Pause.

ASHRAF. We might be a bit tight for money, for a while
anyway, until I get a job –

YASMIN. It's okay. Here.

    She hands him a wadge of cash.

ASHRAF. What is this?

YASMIN. From the er… sewing, and my allowance. I save. It's
time to start on Ashraf Special Sauce Facon Butties properly.
I speak to the fixers on the indoor market – they have space.

ASHRAF. That's a lot of sewing.

YASMIN. Yes. Yes it is.

ASHRAF. Thank you.

Scene Twenty-Seven

The cab has been decked out with ribbons and ASHRAF *is smart in a suit and tie. He waits solemnly.* SHAZIA *enters in a white gown.*

ASHRAF. Habibti. My habibti. Mashallah, you are beautiful.

SHAZIA. Oh shut up, Dad, don't, you'll start me off again!

ASHRAF. No bridesmaids?

SHAZIA. They're at the venue. I thought it'd be nice for you and me to have some time.

Pause.

It looks awesome, Dad.

ASHRAF. Yes – well, it seems Yasmin was doing some moonlighting!

SHAZIA. Er –

ASHRAF. Sewing apparently. It's fine… turns out we're all as crazy as each other. Come.

They get in the cab.

SHAZIA. What's that smell?

ASHRAF. Ashraf's special sauce pie balls – for the guests.

SHAZIA. Great.

She takes the Joop and starts to spray it to cover the smell.

Go on then, crank up the tunes! And put your foot down – Chris hates it when I'm late.

ASHRAF. That bloody cow-licker can wait. He's the luckiest man on God's earth.

SHAZIA. Music please, Dad! And his name is Chris!

ASHRAF *puts on her favourite Arabic tune 'I'm Not a Heathen' and cranks it up.*

I've always loved this one.

ASHRAF. It's in your blood.

A beat.

You know you can still change your mind? Omar still
wanting a wife for his boy.

SHAZIA. Thanks for that, Dad – I do feel way closer to the
culture than I did – thanks to Yas, but I've sort of made my
mind up now.

ASHRAF. Well, you know the prophet said that when you get
married you have completed half of your religion. So I guess
half is better than none!

SHAZIA. Exactly – and to be fair, I'm only half Muslim.

ASHRAF. She would've converted if I'd asked her.

SHAZIA. What, Mum?!

ASHRAF. And that veil is almost a hijab.

SHAZIA. It's all for you, Dad!

They sing along for a bit. ASHRAF *pulls over at the venue.*

ASHRAF. I've got something for you.

SHAZIA. You shouldn't have – you can't aff–

ASHRAF. Shut up, woman! I am your father – respect at all
times! It's for your customs. Something 'old'.

ASHRAF *unchains a thin chain from around his neck, on it
is a ring.*

SHAZIA. What is it?

ASHRAF. It's my wedding ring. To your mother. I hope it
brings you luck.

SHAZIA. Right… 'cause that didn't crash and burn, did it?

ASHRAF. I mean it, habibti! You two will be like the canary
rising from our ashes. Really – we were very happy, we just
made some mistakes. I listened to the wrong people, no
flexible. I wasn't as wise as you, but we loved each other
very much.

He puts the necklace on her.

And if you can't bloody embrace Islam then why don't you bloody embrace Wigan? Your mother made the best Yorkshire puddings I have ever tasted. All you've ever made me is Pot Noodle chicken and mushroom! Some bloody wife you'll be!

SHAZIA. Dad! Language! (*Pause.*) Any more nuggets of wisdom before I go in?

ASHRAF. Yes. Don't be a jacket potato.

SHAZIA. Er, what?

ASHRAF. You heard! Don't be like jacket potato. Sitting around watching *Loose Women* all day. Not good for marriage or career.

SHAZIA. I think you mean couch potato, Dad. You know, on the couch?

ASHRAF. Whatever, work hard, at everything. That's my wisdom for you.

SHAZIA. Thanks.

ASHRAF. Are you okay?

SHAZIA. Bit scared I guess.

ASHRAF. It's okay, habibti. I'll be with you all the way.

SHAZIA. You're walking me?

ASHRAF. Bloody course I am – if those stinking pig racists have taught me anything it's that life is too bloody short for sitting in this car missing the action. And I need to look that cow-licker Kevin in the eye when I give you away. So he knows what's bloody coming to him if he ever steps out of the line. Not that you are my possession to give him of course. You are independent woman just like Beyoncé.

SHAZIA *bursts into tears*.

Don't cry! I joke. I know his name is Chris.

Silence.

SHAZIA. Right. I'm ready.

ASHRAF. Let's go then!

They get out of the car. SHAZIA *takes his arm. He pats the car in a silent goodbye. They walk round the car to the front of the space.*

(*Singing under his breath.*) HERE COMES THE BRIDE, ALL FAT AND WIDE!

SHAZIA *elbows him in the ribs. The cab fades away. Big smiles, the flash of a camera. The music kicks in. Lights.*

A Nick Hern Book

Habibti Driver first published in Great Britain in 2022 as a paperback original by Nick Hern Books Limited, The Glasshouse, 49a Goldhawk Road, London W12 8QP

Habibti Driver copyright © 2022 Shamia Chalabi and Sarah Henley

Shamia Chalabi and Sarah Henley have asserted their right to be identified as the authors of this work

Cover image: photography by The Other Richard and graphic design by Steph Pyne

Designed and typeset by Nick Hern Books, London
Printed in Great Britain by Mimeo Ltd, Huntingdon, Cambridgeshire PE29 6XX

A CIP catalogue record for this book is available from the British Library

ISBN 978 1 83904 084 9

Woodland
CARBON
www.woodlandcarbon.co.uk
NICK HERN BOOKS
Printed on Carbon Captured paper